# NO
# LAUGHING
# MATTER

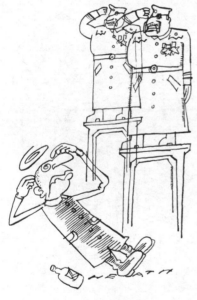

A drunk was rolling around on the ground in front
of a statue of Stalin.

'I'll never drink again,' he wailed, 'I'll never
touch another drop.'

'Why do you say that?' asked a policeman.

'I can see two of them.'

Mao's famous swim in the Yangtze. As he reaches the river bank, the onlookers duly cheer and congratulate him.

'Just a moment,' he says, 'what I want to know first is who pushed me in!'

# NO LAUGHING MATTER

## A Collection of Political Jokes

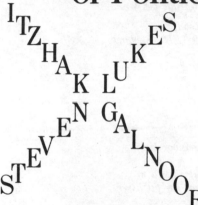

ITZHAK LUKES
STEVEN GALNOOR

Foreword by
**GEORGE MIKES**

Illustrated by
**MICHAEL HEATH**

**ROUTLEDGE & KEGAN PAUL**
London, Boston and Henley

First published in 1985
by Routledge & Kegan Paul plc

14 Leicester Square, London WC2H 7PH, England

9 Park Street, Boston, Mass. 02108, USA and

Broadway House, Newtown Road,
Henley on Thames, Oxon RG9 1EN, England

Set in Plantin
by Columns of Reading
and printed in Great Britain
by T.J. Press (Padstow) Ltd,
Padstow, Cornwall

Library of Congress Cataloging in Publication Data

Lukes, Steven.
No laughing matter.
Includes index.
1. Political satire.   I. Galnoor, Itzhak.   II. Title.
PN6231.P6L85   1985        320'.0207        85-14508

ISBN 0-7100-9965-7

# Contents

# *Foreword*

It's about time that jokes should be taken seriously. Jokes, and particularly political jokes, are the king of minor arts (folksongs, pop music, comics, cartoons etc.). They are minor, no doubt; but equally indubitably they are art, and their historic and social influence raises them high above comics and pop songs.

First a proviso. People who spend long evenings telling one another good or indifferent jokes on the 'Have you heard that one?' -basis belong to the arch-bores of humanity. But, I suppose, looking at El Greco pictures or listening to Beethoven sonatas 22 hours a day would be equally plethoric. Indeed, even the authors of this excellent collection warn us not to sit down and devour their book in one go. Jokes are not a staple diet; they are wonderful spice. You cannot eat salt but food – and life – without salt would be pretty unbearable.

Having said that I have nothing but praise for the political joke. It has, or course, quite a different role in a democracy to that in a totalitarian state. In Britain, for example, a political joke is a joke the subject of which happens to be politics. It needs no greater courage to tell a joke against Mrs Thatcher than to tell one about the English weather. In a tyranny political jokes are acts of defiance and of great courage. Telling a political joke against Big Brother is not only a 'little revolution' as George Orwell (quoted here) called it, but every joke whispered against a regime, every laughter at the expense of the Hitlers and Stalins of this world is a nail in their coffin. Every political joke brings the Great Man down to a human (or inhuman) level; every joke deflates his bombast and megalomania; every joke gives hope and self-confidence to the oppressed. The authors mention that many people in Eastern Europe were imprisoned for telling jokes. I may add that quite a few paid with their lives for a joke or two. Alas, sometimes even for mediocre jokes.

The tyrants know the value and power of jokes only too well. Some of the more intelligent ones realise that jokes are also safety valves. A country where people may joke about their rulers seems to be a free country. In some of the East European countries the Secret Police try to control even the joke output of the population: they invent and spread censored and licenced anti-regime jokes. Some of the Polish and Hungarian leaders were keen on collecting jokes against themselves in the 1960s; Ulbricht of East Germany was keen on collecting the people who told them.

Itzhak Galnoor and Steven Lukes (an Israeli and an Englishman – an excellent combination for the purpose) have shaken one of my firm, old beliefs. I always thought that tyrannies – right or left – were the hotbed of witty, vicious, virulent political jokes while democracies (as I alluded to this earlier) could not and would not create them or, in the best case, regarded political jokes as utterly unimportant. Galnoor and Lukes tend to believe the partial truth of that. The authors remind us that in Poland jokes dried up during the happy days of Solidarity but reappeared with Jaruzelski. I can confirm that during the victorious days of the Hungarian Revolution of 1956 jokes died out, too, but as soon as the Russian tanks started roaring back into the country, causing devastation and death everywhere – while declaring that 'We are coming as friends' – the wits of Budapest retorted: 'A good thing. Imagine how they'd behave if they came as enemies.'

And yet, Lukes and Galnoor are right in pointing out that there are jokey countries and deadly earnest countries. France is no tyranny, neither is Israel, yet political jokes are a way of life in both. East Germany and Bulgaria, on the other hand are not renowned either for their generous liberality or their excellent jokes. (Although Bulgaria is the only country in the world with an officially controlled House of Humour and Satire. Everybody must, I suppose, laugh at all official jokes or else. . . . Well, or else he will be met with the satire of the Secret Police.) Poland and Hungary, on the other hand, have always been making jokes against their rulers and against themselves under all regimes, from Francis Joseph and the Czars to Chernenko. So it seems that oppression alone does not produce good jokes; a sense of humour is needed, too.

And that's where Galnoor and Lukes score splendidly. The jokes they tell are good jokes well told about all sorts of regimes, all over the world. They can be enjoyed simply on the entertainment level. But I wish to congratulate these two eminent academic gentlemen on their thoughts and ideas expressed in the linking texts. Jokes are the folksongs of an urban population and they deserve, I feel, the same serious (though not humourless) attention that Bartók and Kodály gave to the more orthodox type of folk-songs.

George Mikes

# Introduction

A German joke, Mark Twain once said, is no laughing matter. Not only is this in itself rather a good political joke, it also captures one central theme of this collection: that joking about politics is a serious, often a deadly serious business. Joking may often be a release, but in Nazi Germany, in Prague in the early 1950s, or in Santiago more recently it has led to imprisonment. Some of the sources of jokes for this volume specifically asked that we do not thank them by name.

Jokes are a distinctive genre, the products of imagination, typically short stories, imaginative constructs within a realistic setting, communicated orally and thus part of folklore – comparable to, but distinct from, myths, folktales, folksongs, parables and proverbs. They are distinct from anecdotes, which are stories purporting to be true about real events and personalities and pertain to gossip and hearsay: but there is a difference between a sense of humour and a sense of rumour. Jokes involve some kind of unmasking, and belong to the family of satire, parody, caricature, cartoons, etc. but are distinct from all of these. Their effects, when successful, always seem to include some flash of recognition and illumination, understanding and perhaps self-understanding caused by an abrupt switch of a train of thought to a different track. Perhaps, like intuition, a joke achieves this result through a kind of short-cut that avoids reflection and reasoning, though it may well stimulate both. Its essence is a sudden jolt or twist that deflates our expectations and both expresses and releases our anxieties.

What about *political* jokes? Jokes juxtapose apparently incompatible perspectives, and this already is the realm of politics. But the anxieties that political jokes express and release are, in turn, distinctive. They arise from ambiguity and uncertainty, fear and hope, the frustration of expectations and the expectation of frustration. 'Don't talk politics, or else I'm leaving,' grumbles the old man in our first joke. This is what political joking is all about: jokes and politics are both 'public' (that is, affecting anyone you might happen to sit next to on a park bench) and political jokes address a wide array of queries: who are *we* and where do we fit in? On what and on whom can we really rely? How should we interpret the central institutions that shape our lives? How can we respond to arbitrary and repressive power, above all where it claims to liberate us? Which burdens are truly inescapable and how should we adapt to them? Can politics relieve or only increase them?

In short, we interpret the term 'political' in a broad sense, and we do not seek to define it except through our jokes. Freud has told us that in joking there are three partners – the teller, the listener and the target. In political jokes, this last, is a public object, whether a leader, an institution or 'the System' itself. Perhaps we can say that political jokes externalise anxieties about the public domain and the links between what C. Wright Mills called public issues and private troubles.

Popular political jokes reflect a certain level of collective anxiety about public matters. But joking, that is the circulation of political jokes in a society, is a form of coping. Even when the situation is bad, and the jokes become destructive and vicious, they still represent a collective *intimacy*, a sign that people *belong*, that they *care*, and consequently that they entertain *hope*. In a society where the level of political joking is usually high, it may be that the time to worry is when the joking stops. Even the existence of political 'black' humour signals a method of coping. Black or 'gallows' jokes come close to the boundary on the other side of which one finds alienation, total despair and self-hate.

George Orwell referred to political jokes as 'tiny revolutions'. But this is one-sided. They might be subversive or submissive, or both at once. In either case, they are a form of participation, albeit a very passive one, perhaps a substitute for real politics. If that is true, jokes are not a threat to the regime in power. They may reflect opposition and misery but they do not lead to action – to the Big Revolution. This hypothesis may support the rumour that there is indeed a department of the KGB responsible for the production of anti-Soviet jokes. Consequently, in a society with a high level of political jokes, when the joking stops, it could mean that people are busy doing something else. (It is said that in Poland the jokes dwindled as Solidarity grew). People then have neither time nor need to relieve anxiety through political jokes. They have started the Revolution. Alternatively it could mean that they have given up completely.

## The collection

Arthur Koestler has written that analysing humour is at least as delicate as analysing the chemical composition of a perfume – some ingredients are never consciously perceived, while others, when sniffed in isolation, would make us wince. Bearing this advice in mind, we do not here commit the crime of killing our jokes with explanations. Nor do we come to bury them in footnotes: a joke in need of a footnote is a dead joke.

The five hundred or so jokes in this volume have been carefully culled from a larger stock of some three thousand in our filing cabinets. These jokes have been gathered from numerous sources, from dinner parties to scholarly treatises: we have consulted many and stolen from more, including *raconteurs* and humorists, writers on humour and professional historians. We have sought out popular jokes that circulate and so feel under no obligation to document their provenance. Indeed the whole subject of the origin and circulation of political jokes – who invents them and who tells them – remains fascinatingly obscure. George Mikes is doubtless right in attributing a central place to the Central European coffee-house; but the Oriental bazaar, the corridors of power and the prison camp are probably equally significant.

Inevitably, the jokes in this anthology reflect our own tastes (which were remarkably convergent). They are divided into five themes and thirty-one subthemes, according to their political meaning. We hope that the titles are suggestive enough but it is not our fault if there are jokes so richly ambiguous as to defy our classifications.

Clearly, jokes are transferred across boundaries, cultures and generations, and in this process they are also transplanted and reshaped to fit their new environment. We have usually opted for the most 'interesting' version, regardless of contending claims to national parenthood, but we have occasionally indicated alternative versions, where the variations are of interest.

We have concentrated largely on the twentieth century, but the assiduous reader will find examples from Ancient Rome, Medieval Islam and the French Revolution. We should be delighted if this volume were to spur others to collect such jokes from other times and other cultures than are represented here.

One final word of advice to any prospective reader of this volume: *Do not read it*! If you try to follow the King's instructions to the White Rabbit in *Alice in Wonderland* – 'Begin at the beginning, and go on till you come to the end: then stop,' – you will very soon become sated and overcome first with a numbed indifference and then with nausea (as with a box of chocolates – some sweet, some bitter, some hard- and some soft-centred). We advise, rather, judicious sampling.

## Acknowledgements

We are extremely grateful to all those who have responded to our public appeals for material by sending us their cherished jokes, and to all those who have contributed unwittingly to this collection, merely by being convivial or in other ways. Oddly enough, our interest in the subject continues, and we would welcome further jokes, which could be sent to either of us.

Itzhak Galnoor,                     Steven Lukes,
*Political Science Department,*      *Balliol College,*
*Hebrew University,*                 *Oxford,*
*Jerusalem,*                         *England.*
*Israel.*

# 1 *Politics and Joking*

## 1 What is Politics?

*How to define 'politics' is itself an inherently political question. Certainly, there seems to be no non-political way of doing it. Definitions, of course, abound, such as: 'the art of obtaining the money of the rich and the votes of the poor, on the pretext of protecting the one from the other', 'the art of keeping as many balls in the air as possible while protecting your own', and Paul Valéry's – 'the art of preventing people from meddling in their own affairs'. The jokes that follow should help to identify further the broad field with which we are concerned.*

An old man was sitting on a park bench enjoying the sunshine when another old man sat down next to him. They viewed each other cautiously and finally the first one heaved a tremendous sigh. The other one stood up at once and said:
  'Don't talk politics, or else I'm leaving.'

*Other versions:*

Two Jews are travelling in a train between Warsaw and Lodz. Regularly one groans in pain.
  'Oi! oi! oi!'
  The other Jew finally explodes:
  'Can't you do *anything* but talk politics?'

Five citizens of the Reich were sitting in a railway waiting room. One of them sighed, another clasped his head in his hands, the third one groaned loudly and the fourth sat with tears streaming down his face.

The fifth one looked at them, and shook his head.

'Be careful, gentlemen. It's not wise to discuss politics in public.'

\*    \*    \*

A doctor, an engineer and a politician were arguing about which of their professions came first. The doctor pointed out that Eve was created out of Adam's rib – obviously a surgical operation. The engineer countered that the world was created out of chaos – a major feat of engineering.

'Wait a minute,' said the politician, 'the chaos – who do you think was responsible for that?'

A man is vomiting in Prague's Wenceslas Square. Another man comes up to him and says:

'Let me tell you, comrade, I am of the same opinion!'

A mathematics professor sighs:

'All theories are put in question once one gets mixed up in politics. Have you not already noticed that troubles are multiplied by divisions?'

The Cabinet Minister was on his deathbed and the priest was administering the last rites.

'Do you renounce the devil and all his works?' he asked.

'Look here,' said the Cabinet Minister, 'I've always been one for compromise rather than confrontation. Couldn't we achieve some measure of consensus instead?'

At a dinner debate, the French Minister of Finance is questioned by a student.

'M. le Ministre, how can I get into politics?'

'Where does the money in your pocket come from?' asks the Minister.

'Er . . . my father sent it to me.'

'Then be reassured. Once you start spending money that isn't yours, you *are* in politics.'

A British politician turns to a voter and with pride says:

'I'm a self-made man.'

'Apology accepted,' replies the voter.

After uttering the most wounding words, two politicians are reconciled at the behest of their respective friends. They shake hands in front of photographers.

'I wish you,' says the first, 'exactly what you wish me.'

'You see,' the other protests, 'he's beginning again.'

Orator: 'Fellow electors, we must restore the status quo.'

Questioner: 'What does status quo mean?'

Orator: 'It's Latin for the mess we are in.'

Talking to a group of metal-workers, an old French deputy, wanting to be re-elected, proclaims:

'My friends, it's *you* the workers, and you alone, who have made this country what it is.'

'A fine thing!' says one of the workers. 'These guys are extraordinary. They always blame their responsibilities on someone else!'

During an official reception, a guest rushes towards a politician: 'You know,' he says, shaking his hand, 'I've heard a lot about you.'

'But you can't prove any of it,' says the other.

After an all-night meeting between two politicians, eager journalists ask one of them whether the meeting was a success.

'Yes,' he replies, 'We had a real exchange of views. He came in with his views and went out with mine.'

Doctor: 'I'm pleased to tell you that you are the father of triplets.'

Member of Parliament: 'Ridiculous, I demand a recount.'

President Woodrow Wilson, who was out of favour with certain sectors of the Senate and the American public after the First World War, fell ill in 1919. A Senator congratulated him on his recovery, telling him,

'We've all been praying for you.'

'Which way?' asked the President.

'Hasn't he finished yet?' asked the lady who was preparing the tea and biscuits for the MP's annual meeting.

'He finished about half an hour ago,' said the agent, 'but he hasn't stopped yet.'

An American farmer is standing on the steps of the town hall during a political speech. A stranger walks up to him and asks:

'Do you know who's talking in there now or are you just going in?'

'No,' replies the farmer. 'I've just come out and it's Congressman Smith who's talking in there.'

'What's he talking about?' asks the stranger eagerly.

'I don't know. He didn't say!'

A certain Moscow family, fond of telling jokes, owned a parrot. One day it disappeared. They hunted high and low, but it was nowhere to be found. Without wasting any time the owner rushed to the KGB.

'Why come to us?' asked the official in plain clothes, 'We haven't got your parrot. No one's brought it here.'

'Never mind, Comrade Commander, it's bound to be brought in sooner or later and I just want you to know I don't share its opinions.'

A Jew is about to go on a long journey but before his departure he calls on the rabbi and asks him to keep one thousand roubles for him until he returns.

'I'll be delighted to do it,' says the rabbi, 'but money is a serious business, so let me call in my two assistants as witnesses.'

And so the Jew gives him the money in the presence of the two assistants and departs.

After three months the Jew returns, greets the rabbi and asks for his money back.

'One thousand roubles!' cries the rabbi, 'I don't know what you are talking about.'

'I gave it to you three months ago and you even asked your two assistants to be witnesses.'

'In that case,' says the rabbi, 'let's ask them and find out.'

He asks the first assistant, 'Do you know anything about this man's thousand roubles?'

'No,' says the assistant and leaves the room.

The rabbi calls in the second man and repeats the question.

'No,' says the second assistant and leaves the room. The rabbi then goes to his cupboard and takes out the thousand roubles and hands them back.

'But why, rabbi?' asks the Jew.

'Oh, I just wanted to show you what kind of assistants I have.'

---

## 2 Why political jokes?

*Why do people tell political jokes? What needs do they satisfy? What social functions do they fulfil? And who tells them and to whom? How do they spread? Are they largely an elite phenomenon, more at home in clubs than pubs, in coffee-houses than canteens? Do they travel more easily from Whitehall to the White House than from Whitehall to Whitechapel? And where and when do they flourish?*

*Under authoritarian and repressive regimes, it is sometimes suggested. Political jokes are obviously better enjoyed where they are forbidden or where telling them is dangerous, but there are authoritarian states with little underground humour (so far as we know) and non-authoritarian states with hilarious political jokes. Being oppressed does not guarantee a sense of political humour; and many non-democratic regimes have not produced (or perhaps have not exported?) political jokes. On the other hand, some democracies, such as Ireland, Italy, Israel and France, are richly stocked.*

*Perhaps the answer is that they flourish in settings where politics is pervasive and there is a relatively high level of anxiety about politics and its effects on daily life. This is a good starting-point for explaining the appearance of political joking in Nazi-controlled Denmark and Norway, or the sudden waning of political jokes in societies where they were previously abundant. It also enables us carefully to circumvent the offensive question whether some cultures are more disposed to produce and consume political jokes than others.*

A prison camp.

A newcomer observes the inmates telling political jokes. All the jokes are by now so deeply familiar that they simply refer to them by number.

'Forty three,' says one. General hilarity.

'Two hundred and three,' says a second. Appreciative chuckles.

'Three hundred and twenty nine,' says a third. The assembled company dissolves in hysterics.

The newcomer decides to try his hand. 'Ninety-one,' he ventures. Total silence. He tries again: 'Three hundred and one.' Not a titter. 'Forty-two.' A deathly hush. Puzzled, he asks his heighbour what he did wrong.

'Nothing,' he says. 'It's just the way you tell them.'

President Nasser was furious when some of the 'Nuktas' (jokes) making their rounds in Egypt reached him.

'Track down the author of these stories,' he shouts to his security guards. Soon enough a frail old man is brought before the President.

'Aren't you ashamed of spreading these lying jokes about your country and your President? Isn't it unbecoming in a man of your years?'

The old man said nothing.

'Here I am, trying to build this wonderful country, instituting agrarian reform, spreading the rule of law, fighting for justice, for equality, for the happiness of all our people . . .'

The old man interrupts him:

'Excuse me, Mr. President, but I swear to Allah that that joke isn't mine.'

*Other versions:*

As soon as Hitler came into power and before he had the chance to put his plans into effect, the country was deluged by anti-Nazi jokes. He was furious and ordered that whoever was responsible for these jokes be brought to him personally. Several weeks later, police arrested Kaufmann, a Jewish critic.

'What's your name, Jew?' asked Hitler.

'Kaufmann.'

'Are you responsible for the joke about me and the pig?'

'Yes.'

'What about the joke in which whenever I die will be a Jewish holiday?'

'Yes, that one's mine.'

'What about the joke in which I'm saved from drowning and when I offer the Jew who saved me a reward, his request is simply that I don't tell anyone what he did?'

'Oh yes, that one is also mine.'

'Jew, how dare you make these jokes? How dare a Jew be so impudent? Don't you know who I am? The leader of the Third Reich, which is destined to last 1000 years!'

'Now wait a minute,' says Kaufmann, 'Don't blame me for that joke – I never heard it before!'


Khruschev was furious with the joke tellers:

'It's a disgrace! Jokes and then more jokes! Who makes them up? Bring me just one joke writer!'

They bring a joke writer to him. The joke writer pauses in the doorway of Khruschev's home and looks around, with great admiration.

'What are you looking for?' Khruschev asks him.

'I'm just looking. I see that you don't live too badly.'

'Well what of it? In twenty years we'll have Communism and everybody will live like this!' says Khruschev.

'Aha!' says the joke writer. 'A new joke!'


★　　★　　★


A conversation between Walter Ulbricht and Willy Brandt:

'Have you a hobby, Herr Brandt?'

'Yes, I collect jokes that people tell about me,' says

Brandt. 'And you?'

'Oh, I collect people who tell jokes about me,' says Ulbricht.


During a break in the summit meeting in Helsinki, President Carter asked Brezhnev whether he collected stories against himself.

'I certainly do,' replied Brezhnev.

'Do you have many?' asked Carter.

'Two camps full,' said Brezhnev.


An Englishman, a German and a Russian were arguing together over which of their three nations was the bravest. ·

'We're the bravest,' insisted the Englishman, 'because one in every ten of us is drowned at sea.'

'Nonsense,' protested the German. 'We are the bravest, because one in every six of us dies on the battlefield.'

'You are both wrong,' said the Russian. '*We* are the bravest, because although every second one of us is an informer, we still tell political jokes.'


Two men were talking together over a drink:

'Have you heard the rumour that Brezhnev is ill?'

'No.'

'Nor have I. But if we could start it going . . . .'


'Have you hard the news? *Pravda* is going to hold a competition for the best political joke.'

'What's the first prize?'

'Twenty years.'


A small, feeble man, walking along the street in Armenia, meets a huge, muscular giant of a man, a veritable Goliath, who socks him in the jaw. The small man is inclined to hit back, but hesitates. 'Hey,' he says. 'Was that serious, or was it a joke?'

'It was serious,' says the big man.

'Oh, good,' says the small man, 'I never did like jokes.'


At a board meeting, a new director, looking at the solemn faces around the table, decided to liven up the proceedings by telling a South African Van der Merwe joke. It worked well, and all the other directors dissolved in laughter, except one, who looked very sour.

'Oh, dear,' thought the new member, 'that chap's name must be Van der Merwe.'

'Excuse me,' he asked, 'but is your name Van der Merwe?'

'Yes it is,' snapped the other.

'Oh, I *am* sorry, I'll tell it again – slowly.'


An American diplomat tells a joke in a public meeting in an African state. He takes his time and tells the joke very slowly and at great length. Eventually he finishes and the interpreter translates in a few words and a roar of laughter breaks out.

'How did you manage to tell the joke so briefly?' asks the diplomat.

'Oh,' says the interpreter, 'I just said: he told a joke. Laugh!'


In a totalitarian country, two men were standing together in the corridor of a train surreptitiously making strange hand movements under their coats.

'Look at those two,' said one passenger to another.

'What are they up to?'

'Don't worry, they're deaf-and-dumb. They're telling each other political jokes.'

# 2  Boundaries and Identity

*The jokes in this part all, in varying ways, concern division and uncertainty – uncertainty created by divisions, whose contours may be unclear (whom can I trust?) or all too clear (as in 'ethnic' jokes). The uncertainty concerns both the reality and the appearance of identity: who am I? who are you? who are we? who are they? how do we appear to one another? The differences alluded to can be between states, nations, ethnic groups, localities and even gods.*

*These jokes are marvellously ambiguous in mixing self-confidence with the need for reassurance, and pride with envy. They also seem to be particularly nervy – and to touch particularly raw nerves. We have, however, exercised one strict prohibition: we have rigorously excluded all crude insults (though we have included some subtler jokes that trade on them). The reason is simple: they aren't particularly funny and they are all basically identical. Moreover, including them would probably have caused great offence, leading to legal suits if not physical violence on the part of insulted parties.*

## 1 Trust and mistrust

In Franco's days, two Spanish border guards were patrolling the frontier between Spain and France.

'What would you do if I was suddenly to make a run for it?' asked one of them, gazing longingly towards France. 'Would you shoot?'

'Yes,' answered the other. 'Wouldn't you?'

'No.'

'In that case, I'll go first.'

Two Czechs stand in a street, admiring a brand new Cadillac parked outside an hotel in Prague.

'What a fantastic achievement of Soviet technology!' says the first.

'Soviet technology?' says the other, 'Don't you *know* that this is an American car?'

'Yes of course I do,' says the first, 'but I don't know you.'

An American journalist asks Admiral Carrero Blanco, Vice-President of the Spanish government, 'In all frankness, what do you think of General Franco?'

The admiral makes a gesture of fear. Putting a finger to his lips, he leads the journalist out of his office. They get into his car and he tells his driver to drive out of town. In silence all the while, they drive to a deserted spot, in the middle of a desolate sierra. The admiral makes the journalist get out and they walk for a further hour into the mountain, At last the admiral, feeling free from indiscreet ears, whispers in the journalist's ear, 'Between ourselves, I rather like him.'

An Austrian Communist receives his call-up papers and knows he is to be sent to the Eastern front where he will have to fight his comrades. So he tries to get himself arrested. He goes into the countryside and first finds a peasant whom he addresses with the words 'Heil Moscow!'. The peasant responds by saying, 'You poor fellow! You'll get into terrible trouble if you go round saying that sort of thing,' and offers him a meal.

He next finds a policeman whom he similarly greets with 'Heil Moscow!'. 'Shut up, you fool,' says the policeman, 'Do you want to get me into trouble?'

Finally, he sees a whole platoon of SS men coming round the corner and yells 'Heil Moscow!'. 'Be quiet, you idiot!' the commanding officer hisses at him, 'there's a Nazi in the fourth row.'

Two friends meet in a Warsaw tram. One asks the other a riddle:

'What difference is there between a serviette and the Government?' His friend shrugs, so he explains:

'A serviette is used to wipe one's mouth, but the Government is only good for wiping one's bottom.'

At which a third pasenger enters the game.

'And what difference is there between you and the conductor?'

The two friends can't think of an answer. Then the stranger shows them his police identity card and declares:

'The conductor is going to the terminus, but as for you, you are getting off with me at the next stop.'

At once, the author of the first riddle protests that he certainly didn't mean the Polish government.

'Yes, you did,' says the policeman, 'I have been in the police force for fifteen years and I am better placed than anyone to know which government is good for wiping one's bottom.'

The up-and-coming local Party Secretary could not help noticing that the Party Chairman, an influential person at higher levels, always fell asleep while he was giving the Secretary's report.

One day he plucked up the courage to mention it to him.

'Comrade Chairman, I cannot help noticing that you always fall asleep during my reports. Do you not have confidence in me?'

'Of course I do. Would I fall asleep if I didn't?'


A citizen in Budapest after the invasion in 1956 goes to the police station and complains:

'My Russian watch has been stolen by a Swiss soldier.'

'Haven't you got it mixed up?' asks the policeman.

'Only if you insist,' responds the Hungarian.


Chou En Lai and Brezhnev are on a hunting trip, in China. As they creep through the forest they spot a tiger, and simultaneously fire and kill it. Brezhnev tells Chou En Lai to watch the tiger while he goes to get somebody to help them carry it off. Ten minutes later, he returns, but Chou is standing there alone, no tiger.

'Where's the tiger?' asks Brezhnev.

'What tiger?' replies Chou.

'Wait a minute, didn't we come out here to hunt animals?'

'Yes, we did.'

'And didn't we both see a tiger?'

'Yes, we did.'

'And didn't we both shoot the tiger?'

'Yes, we did.'

'And didn't I leave you here alone and ask you to guard the tiger for a few minutes?'

'Yes you did.'

'So where's the tiger?'

'What tiger?'

A telephone conversation in Bucharest:
'How are you?'
'I'm fine.'
'Is everything well?'
'Everything is perfect.'
'Are you *sure?*'
'I am *very happy.*'
'Sorry, I didn't realize that you had company.'


A Pole comes into a Warsaw bank.
'I have 100 zlotys,' says the Pole, 'I can't decide what would be the safest thing to do with them.'
'Put them in a bank,' says the bank clerk.
'But what if the bank crashes?' says the Pole.
'If the bank crashes then the bank administration guarantees to refund your money,' replies the clerk.
'Well, what if the administration goes bust?'
'Then the Polish Ministry of Finance guarantees to refund your money.'
'What if the Finance Ministry goes bust?'
'Then the Polish government guarantees to refund your money.'
'What if the Polish government goes bankrupt?'
'Well, in that case the friendly Soviet Union guarantees the return of your money.'
'And what if the Soviet Union goes bankrupt?'
'You don't mean to say you'd begrudge 100 zlotys for that?'


'What are you in for?' one prisoner asks another.
'I was lazy.'
'Do you mean you engaged in sabotage?'
'No, I was having a chat with a friend of mine about the political situation. I thought I could wait until morning before denouncing him. He managed to get to the Security Police the same night.'

In an overcrowded Lisbon bus in the days of Salazar's dictatorship, a passenger taps another on the shoulder and asks politely:

'Excuse me, Señor, are you a member of the armed forces?'

'No,'

'Is your father, or anyone else in your family a member of the armed forces?'

'No,'

'Are you a police officer?'

'No,'

'Perhaps a Government official?'

'No,' says the man, getting very irritated.

'Are you sure that you and your family are not connected in any way with the Government?'

'No!!'

'In that case, get off my bloody foot!'

The chief of the Secret Police of a Latin American dictatorship goes to a barber:

'Do you know who I am?' he asks.
'No,' says the barber.
'Perfect, in that case, you can shave me.'

---

## 2 Appearance and reality

After a wave of petty theft of state property, security guards were posted outside all Soviet factories. The attention of one such guard, standing watch outside the Joseph Stalin timber works in Leningrad, fell upon Pyotr Petrovich, who was passing through the gates with a bulky and suspicious-looking sack perched on a wheelbarrow.

'What's in that sack, Pyotr?' asked the guard.

'Sawdust and shavings. The foreman said I could take them home.'

'I wasn't born yesterday, you know. Come on, empty it out.'

Grumbling, Pyotr emptied the sack. Sure enough, it was full of sawdust and shavings.

The next day, the same thing happened again.

'Come on, empty it out,' ordered the guard.

But once again it contained nothing but sawdust and shavings.

The same thing happened day after day. Day after day Pyotr emptied his sack, shovelled it all back in again, and bundled it off home.

Finally the guard's sense of duty was vanquished by his growing curiosity.

'Look here, Pyotr,' he said, 'I *know* you're stealing something. But I promise you I'll never bother you again, you can take what you like if you only tell me *what* it is you're stealing.'

'Wheelbarrows, my friend, wheelbarrows.'


A drunk was rolling around on the ground in front of a statue of Stalin.

'I'll never drink again,' he wailed, 'I'll never touch

another drop.'

'Why do you say that?' asked a policeman.

'I can see two of them.'

A peasant has applied for membership of the Communist Party. The Party secretary first asks him a few questions:

'Comrade, if the Party were to ask you for a donation of a hundred roubles, would you comply unhesitatingly?'

'Yes.'

'And if the Party were to request you to enlist your only son in the Red Army?'

'I would enlist him.'

'What if the Party were to ask you to donate your cow to help in the fight against the White armies? Would you do so?'

'No.'

'Do you mean to tell me that you would give a

hundred roubles or an only son, but not a cow?'
'But comrade, I *have* a cow.'


A teacher was reading fairy stories to a class of children
in post-revolutionary Russia. Without thinking he read:
'. . . and God gave the raven a piece of cheese.'
A small boy jumped to his feet and protested: 'There
is no such thing as God!'
The teacher took fright, but quickly retrieved the
situation.
'And cheese?' he said, 'Is there such a thing as
cheese? As you now see, both references were purely
symbolic.'

*Another version:*

A Russian inspector was checking in a collective farm.
'How's the turnip crop?' he asked.
'Ah,' said the manager enthusiastically, 'under our
inspired plan we are growing so many turnips that if
they were piled up all together they would form a
mountain reaching to the feet of God.'
'But you know,' said the inspector, 'that there is no
God.'
'No,' said the manager, 'and there are no turnips
either.'

\*     \*     \*

At the 20th Congress of the Communist party of the
Soviet Union the delegate from Kazakhstan fell asleep
during Khruschev's speech.
Just after Khruschev launched into his attack on Stalin
the speech was interrupted by the comrade from
Kazakhstan who cried in his sleep:
'Khruschev is a liar, a traitor and a monster!'
A terrific silence fell on the hall. The delegate sitting
next to him jabbed the comrade in the ribs, waking him
up and whispered:
'What are you saying? Don't you know you're at the

20th Party Congress?'

'I'm sorry, I must have dozed off,' the comrade from Kazakhstan confessed, 'I was dreaming that I was at the 21st Congress.'

A Russian returns to his native town after a long absence. On his way through town he notices a large statue of Petrov who invented the telephone, the electric light-bulb, the aeroplane, the cuckoo clock and many other important things. He continues walking and comes upon an even larger statue of Ivanov.

'Who's Ivanov?' he asks.

'Ivanov,' he is told, 'Ivanov invented Petrov.'

*Another version:*

A Soviet athlete chats, during a tournament in San Francisco, with an American competitor.

'Who is the greatest man in the USSR?' the latter asks.

'Oh,' says the Russian, 'I'm tempted to say Popov. He invented electricity, radio, television, the submarine, the helicopter, the electric coffee-mill and the atomic bomb. But he is not as great as Pronchkine.'

'Why? What did Pronchkine do?'

'He invented Popov.'

\*   \*   \*

A Hungarian walked into a Budapest hospital and asked for the eye and ear section. A nurse tells him that the sections have been separated.

'Oh, but I must go to both. In the last few years I don't know what's happened to me. I don't see what I hear and I don't hear what I see.'

The teacher is asking a class of children what their parents do for a living. It is little Ferenc's turn to answer.

'My dad works as doorkeeper in a Budapest brothel,' he says.

The teacher is horrified. She sends a note to Ferenc's father asking him to come in and see her.

The next day he drops in, in the uniform of an AVO (secret police) major.

'But Comrade Major,' stammers the teacher. 'Your son Ferenc told me you were a doorkeeper in a brothel!'

'He always says that,' says the major. 'He's ashamed of people knowing.'

A clerk in a Rumanian ministry is sitting around drinking coffee. A man walks in and starts to complain about the slow service he's been getting.

'Look,' says the bureaucrat, 'our country pretends to pay us, so we pretend to work.'

A man goes into a Warsaw shop after the ending of Jaruzelski's emergency rule and asks for a copy of the Polish constitution.

'Shall I wrap it for you?' asks the sales assistant, 'or will you tear it up now?'

Two Jews were walking down the street in Nazi Germany, when they came upon a public notice. 'ESCAPED! A lion has escaped from the Berlin Zoo. The animal is to be shot on sight.'

'That's it!' said the first man. 'I'm leaving town tonight.'

'What are you talking about?' asked the second. 'You're not a lion.'

'No,' said the first. 'But try to tell them that after you've been shot!'

Khruschev dies and is sent to hell, but as a special courtesy he is escorted around the chambers and is given a choice. In the first chamber he sees people burning in fire; he runs to the second chamber and there he sees flogging and torture; in the third everyone is chained . . . He is about to give up when he sees a nice room and when he peeps through the key-hole he sees Stalin seated on a comfortable chair with Marilyn Monroe on his lap.

'That's the place for me! cries Khruschev.

'Son,' says the accompanying angel, 'That's *her* hell, not his.'

Ben Gurion dies and is sent down to hell. On arrival he is escorted around hell. He's taken through green fields, orchards, lakes, he meets friendly people, and is all in all surprised with the pleasant surroundings. Unfortunately the devil receives a message and tells Ben Gurion that God wants him in heaven. Ben Gurion goes to heaven and as soon as he gets there he asks to see God. He gets an audience with God and asks him if he can go back to hell.

'Look,' says Ben Gurion, 'it was really beautiful there. I'd like to stay.'

'Well,' says God, 'It's very irregular, but since you are Ben Gurion, I'll let you go.'

He's sent back down to hell, and he sees that it's not the same as before. It's now smelly, smoggy, dirty, the people are rude, in short it's very unpleasant. He goes up to the Devil and says:

'Look. I was here a while ago, and it was really beautiful, now it's horrible, what happened?'

'Easy,' says the Devil, 'last time you were a tourist, now you're a resident.'

An Israeli sentry stopped two individuals toiling up a rocky road. One was a woman, obviously pregnant, seated on a donkey. By her side was an elderly man, trudging along on foot.

'Hold it! Where are you going?' demanded the sentry.

'To Bethlehem!' said the elderly man wearily.

'Your name?' said the sentry.

'Joseph!'

At this point the sentry paused. 'Is this woman your wife?'

'Yes, she is.'

'Is her name Mary?'

The elderly man looked surprised.

'Why, yes. How did you know?'

The sentry paused a long time now. He said, 'Listen, are you planning to name your child Jesus?'

The elderly man said, in even greater surprise,

'Why, yes. How did you know?'

Nervously, the sentry stepped back and in a deeply troubled whisper said,

'Well, move on! Go on to Bethlehem!'

The man and his pregnant wife proceeded along the road for several hundred yards and then the man turned to the woman and said, softly,

'It seems to have worked, Fatima. For some reason, that Israeli thought we were Puerto Ricans.'


In 1949 at a mathematical congress in the USSR, the President reads out a message from Stalin: 'Two plus two equals six.'

A mathematician, however, insists in his presentation that two plus two equals four. He is sent to Siberia. Six years later he is rehabilitated and attends another Congress, at which the President sends out a message from Khruschev: 'Two plus two equals five.'

The mathematician delivers his speech again insisting that two plus two equals four. He is taken aside by the KGB men who remonstrate with him:

'Look, we aren't intellectuals. We know as well as you do that two plus two equals four. But under Stalin they equalled six, under Khruschev five – that's progress isn't it?'

In England, everything is permitted, except what is expressly forbidden.

In the USSR, everything is forbidden, save what is expressly permitted.

In France, everything is permitted, even what is expressly forbidden.

In China, everything is forbidden, even what is expressly permitted.

What is the difference between a materialist, an idealist and a marxist?

A materialist is in a dark room, chasing a non-existent black cat and he knows there is no cat.

An idealist is in a dark room, chasing a non-existent black cat and he believes there is a cat.

A marxist is in a dark room, chasing a non-existent black cat, and he keeps finding it.

A distinguished Soviet aesthetician was answering questions on the theory of art.

'What is expressionism?' one questioner asked.

'Expressionism is painting what you feel.'

'What is impressionism?'

'Impressionism is painting what you see.'

'And what is socialist realism?'

'Socialist realism is painting what you hear.'

One day General Alfredo Stroessner was making a surprise inspection of towns in the Paraguayan country-side. He happened to enter the small hamlet of Curuguaty and found it as sleepy as ever. Entering the local drinking establishment, he soon discovered that a goodly number of the town's inhabitants were spending their day getting drunk. The General took a seat, ordered a beer, and awaited the adulation that usually accompanied his appearance. He waited and waited. Yet no one stepped forward to recognize him despite his uniform. Finally, he could wait no longer and he blurted out,

'What's the matter with you people? My name is on every street of the nation and nobody here recognizes me.' Hearing this, one of the drunks stepped forward, his hand outstretched.

'I can't tell you how glad I am to meet you, Señor Coca-Cola!'

### 3 Us and them: ethnic differences

An Israeli prisoner of war comes back from Egypt.
  'It was terrible,' he tells his friends.
  'What was so terrible? The food?'
  'No.'
  'Were you beaten?'
  'No.'
  'The interrogation?'
  'No.'

'So?'
'They tied my hands and I couldn't speak.'

A census was conducted in Poland after World War I and a Jewish student was asked to fill in a form. When he reached the clause about 'nationality', he hesitated for a moment and wrote down 'Jewish'. The clerk became very annoyed and told him:
'You are in Poland and you are a Polish citizen; so why do you write "Jewish"?'
'You see,' said the student, 'my parents are in Berlin and they are Germans; my brother is in Petersburg and he is Russian; my second brother lives in Bucharest and he is Rumanian; my sister in Paris is French and my other sister is English. My uncle is a merchant in Budapest and he is a Hungarian; his brother, my other uncle, is in The Hague and carries a Dutch passport; so I thought to myself, in such a big family, there is also room for one Jew.'

*The next two jokes form an intriguing pair:–*

Two Poles met in Cracow in 1950. The one notices that the other looks exceedingly prosperous and asks,
'How come you look so well off when you don't have a job?'
'It's simple', says the other, 'I'm hiding a family of rich Jews.'
'But it's five years since the end of the war!'
'Yes, but *they* don't know that.'

Two Jews meet in Warsaw in 1968.
'Rosenberg,' says the first, 'They tell me that you have lost your job and yet you look well, happy and prosperous. How is this? What are you living on?'
'I'm living by blackmail,' the other replies.
'By blackmail? How come?'
'It's very simple. There is a Polish family that hid me

during the war against the Nazis.'
'So?'
'I'm blackmailing them.'

A few months after the end of World War I, the Premier of Poland had a meeting with President Woodrow Wilson.

'If you don't meet our nation's demands at the peace conference,' warned the Premier, 'I foresee great troubles ahead. The Polish people will be very angry and they'll go out and massacre the Jews!'

'And if your demands *are* met?' asked Wilson.

'In that case,' replied the Premier, 'my people will be delighted. They'll go out into the streets and get drunk – and then they'll massacre the Jews!'

A Jew applied for a job as a postman in Moscow.
'Can you read English, French, German and Russian?'
'Yes I can.'
'Can you play a the trumpet?'
'Yes I can.'
'Can you ride a bicycle?'
'Yes I can.'
'Then we can't employ you. We want someone who can't ride a bicycle.'

It is winter. A rumour goes around that there has been a meat delivery. A huge line forms outside the butcher's shop. After three hours have passed the shop door opens and the manager announces:

'Friends, we have meat but not enough for everyone; would the Jews please leave.'

The Jews leave; the line gets shorter.

Two hours later the door opens again:

'Comrades, we have meat but not enough for everyone. Would all those who didn't take part in the Great Patriotic War please leave.'

Three hours later the door opens again: 'Comrades, we have meat but not enough for everyone. Would all those who didn't take part in the overthrow of Tsarism please leave.'

There are now only three half frozen old men left. At eight o'clock the door opens once more: 'Comrades, there won't be any meat.'

The old men move off grumbling: 'The Jews always get the best of everything!'

The Chief Rabbi of Moscow dies and Stalin demands to know the names of all the candidates for the post. An official of the KGB hands him a list, and Stalin begins to read: Abramovitch . . . Isaakimov . . . Rubinstein . . . Simeonovitch . . .

Stalin jumps to his feet.

'What's the meaning of this? All these men are Jews . . .'

A deputation from the Jews of Strasbourg seeks an audience with the town's commandant.

'Throw them out,' he orders. 'These villains murdered our Lord and Saviour!'

'But Sir,' says an officer, 'I hear they've brought a lot of money for the treasury.'

'Ah well,' grunts the commandant, 'let them in – after all, they didn't know what they were doing.'

One day a young black man showed up at the gates of heaven and was met by St Peter.

'I'd like to be admitted into heaven, St Peter.'

'Fine, but first tell me what you've done lately which would permit you to be admitted.'

'Well, I marched from Selma to Montgomery Alabama in a civil rights march.'

'You know a lot of people marched in the march from Selma to Montgomery. Maybe there is something else?'

'Yes, I got married on the courthouse steps in Montgomery at noon.'

'What's so unusual about that?'

'I married a white woman.'

St Peter's eyes widen. 'You married a white woman on the courthouse steps in Montgomery Alabama at twelve o'clock noon? When was that?'

'Oh, about two minutes ago.'


An old southern colonel had returned to his home in Virginia after a long absence. He called on an old friend and enquired if there had been any changes in the local political scene in his absence.

'Well,' answered the friend, 'There has been one big change; the legislature has passed making it a crime to shoot a nigger.'

'You don't say,' cried the Colonel in amazement. 'In what month?'


A rich white woman and her black maid give birth to babies at the same time. Some months later, proud of her child's progress, the white woman rushes into her kitchen, saying,

'He's just said his first word.'

'Oh really,' says the black baby from his cot, 'what did he say?'


A Jew and a black are sitting opposite one another in the New York subway. To his astonishment, the Jew sees that the black man is reading a newspaper in Yiddish. Finally he leans over and asks:

'Are you *Jewish*?'

'Look man,' says the black, 'Give me a break.'


The South African Van der Merwe parks his little Volkswagen in the street and goes to do some shopping.

When he returns, he finds an enormous Cadillac parked in front of his car and a plush Rolls Royce behind – each so close to his car that he can't move.

'These rich bloody Jews,' he fumes, 'with all their bloody money they think they can do as they damned well like.'

Just then the driver of the Cadillac arrives and Van der Merwe rages at him.

'By the way,' asks Van der Merwe, 'what's your name?'

'Van Tonder,' said the Cadillac owner.

Van der Merwe is a little taken aback, but at that moment the owner of the Rolls arrives, so he tells him off as well.

'By the way,' said Van der Merwe, 'what's *your* name?'

'Van Zyl.'

Exasperated, Van der Merwe screams at both of them: 'It's people like you who are giving the Jews a bad name.'


Van der Merwe and Van Tonder were walking around in London and they stopped to watch some men working in the street. After a while Van Tonder shook his head and said,

'Why do they need so many people to do this job?'

Van der Merwe nodded in agreement.

'Wragtig,' he said, 'it's amazing. Just give me six boys and I could do it by myself.'


At a late-night party in Paris, some playful Frenchmen got Van der Merwe into a corner and asked him whether love-making was regarded as work or play in South Africa. Van der Merwe thought about this for a while and then slowly answered that it was play.

'Why did it take you so long to make up your mind, Van?' one asked.

'Well, gentlemen,' replied Van der Merwe, 'it must

be play because if it was work, we'd get our Blacks to
do it.'


Mr. Vorster was doing a nationwide tour by helicopter,
visiting constituents, farmers and construction workers
in out-of-way places. Flying over the Limpopo River he
looked down and saw two white men in a motor boat,
towing a black man behind them on water-skis.
'Hell,' said Mr. Vorster, 'and they tell me there's no
detente going on inside the country. Go lower, pilot, I
want to talk to these men.'
He pulled out his loud-hailer.
'Men,' he shouted, 'I want you to know that it makes me
proud to see co-operation between the races like this.
Keep it up.'
And with a signal to his pilot, away he flew.
Down in the boat, a puzzled Van der Merwe turned
to his friend.
'Mr Vorster's a good ou,' he said, 'But he doesn't
know much about crocodile hunting.'


An Indian enters a hotel to book a room in the mid-west
in the U.S.
'Just put your cross here,' says the receptionist.
The Indian puts two crosses.
'What is the second cross for?' asks the receptionist.
'Oh, that's my Ph.D. from Harvard.'


An American Indian paid a visit to New York. While
shopping in a drug store, he got into conversation with
the storekeeper, who asked:
'And how do you like our city?'
'Fine,' replied the Indian. 'And how do you like our
country?'


A little American Indian boy and a little black boy were

arguing together about which of their two peoples was tops.

'We've got all the best boxers,' said the black boy. 'We've got all the best athletes. We've got the best music. We've got black politicians and black mayors. But you Indians ain't got nothing at all.'

'We got Geronomo,' said the Indian boy. 'And we got Sitting Bull too.'

'That's nothing. That was years ago. What you got now?'

The Indian boy thought for a while, and then said:

'You think you're pretty smart. But how many times you seen them white kids playing cowboys and blacks?'


Heard in the United States:

'How do you tell the Polish guy at a cockfight?'

'He brings a duck.'

'How do you tell the Italian guy?'

'He bets on the duck.'

'How do you tell the Mafia is there?'

'The duck wins.'


Van der Merwe was walking down a street in Belfast when he felt the barrel of a gun thrust into his back.

'Protestant or Catholic?' a voice demanded.

Van had to think fast.

'I am Jewish,' he said.

'Then I must be the luckiest Arab in Belfast.'


One of the first black members of a U.S. administration was out one morning mowing his lawn in a fashionable area of Washington. A white lady is passing by and, taking him for a hired gardener, asks if he would come around one afternoon and mow her lawn.

He: 'My services are not for sale.'

She: 'So why are you mowing the lawn?'

He: 'I sleep with the lady of the house.'

Kreif van der Merwe is making his first visit to Pretoria since Zimbabwe gained its freedom. He is scandalized by one sight in the street and asks the man standing next to him:
'Tell me, was that P.W. Botha in the black limousine that just passed here?'
'Of course it was.'
'I haven't seen him since our school days. What great company is he running nowadays?'
'Company? He's the Prime Minister now.'
'Prime Minister!' exclaims Van der Merwe, 'Up in Zimbabwe, that's kaffir work these days.'

---

## 4 Him, us and them: religious differences

A Dublin Jew collapses in the street and is on the point of death. A priest, who happens to be passing by, takes the man in his arms and says:
'Do you believe in God the Father, the Son and the Holy Ghost?'
The Jew opens one eye and croaks:
'Here I am dying, and he asks me riddles.'

Paddy, the Irishman, who was on his death-bed, let it be known that he had decided to renounce Catholicism and become a Protestant.
When the village priest heard of Paddy's sudden conversion, he hurried over to see him:
'What in God's name made you do it, Paddy?'
'Me time is up, Father. So I said to meself: if anyone's got to die, then let it be one of those Protestant Orange bastards . . .'

An American tourist finds himself in Belfast on the 12th of July, on the occasion of the annual ceremonies commemorating the victory of King William at the Boyne. Puzzled by the banners that are being carried and the anthems that are being sung, he decides to find out a little more about what is going on. He stops the next bowler-hatted figure to cross his path and asks:

'Say, old-timer, who exactly was this King Billy?'

The Orangeman gives him a withering look before brusquely replying: 'Ach away mon and read your Bible.'

Tenders are invited for the building of a new church. A Jewish architect is among those submitting plans.

'But you are not of our faith,' the priest objects.

'We are more or less,' counters the Jew. 'As for Jesus preaching and healing the sick, even I believe that. And as for him resurrecting the dead, my draughtsman believes that. I also believe that Jesus suffered and died on the cross. And my draughtsman believes that he rose from the dead. Neither would I contest the fact that his mother's name was Mary. As for her being a virgin, well, I'm not quite sure whether my draughtsman believes that or not . . . But the firm believes it.'

An Orthodox priest, a Catholic priest and a rabbi are talking about how much of the collection they give God, and how much they keep for themselves.

'I divide all the money coming into the church into a big pile and a small pile; the big one is for God and the small one is for me,' says the Orthodox priest.

'Well,' says the Catholic priest, 'I divide the money into two even piles, one for God and one for me.'

'I put all the money on a tray and throw it up into the air,' says the rabbi. 'And what God wants God keeps.'

The Pope has died and goes to heaven. St Peter asks him whom among the saints he would like to meet.

'Saint Mary, the mother of Jesus Christ,' says the Pope.

Peter leads him into a palatial hall. There, in a far

corner, sits an old Jewish lady. The Pope approaches her reverently and sinks to his knee.

'O Holy Mother of God,' he says, 'all my life on earth I have been looking forward to this blessed moment. There is one question I want to ask you – what was it like to give birth to our Lord Jesus Christ?'

The old Jewish lady wags her head and smiles: 'Vell, ectually ve vanted a little girl . . .'

A Jew goes into a Belfast pub and is immediately asked: 'Are you a Catholic or a Protestant?'

'I'm a Jew,' he says.

'But are you a Catholic Jew or a Protestant Jew?'

A few years ago, when Catholic church reform began to be much in the news, Mrs Moskowitz said to Mrs Finkelstein, 'Tell me, Becky, have you by any chance heard what's going on in Rome?'

'No', said Mrs. Finkelstein. 'I haven't. What's going

on in Rome?'

'A meeting of high Catholic churchmen has, among other things, decided that the Jews are not responsible for the crucifixion of Jesus'.

Mrs. Finkelstein raised her eyebrows. 'Indeed. And who *is* responsible, then?'

'I'm not sure,' said Mrs. Moskowitz. 'I think they suspect the Puerto Ricans.'

A young Irish girl was talking to the Reverend Mother about her ambitions in life.

'When I grow up,' she announced, 'I want to be a prostitute.'

The Reverend Mother gasped and threw up her hands in horror.

'Did I hear you rightly? What was it you said you wanted to be?'

'A prostitute.'

Reverend Mother sighed with relief.

'O Praise the Lord!', she said, 'I thought you said a Protestant!'

The Medici Pope, Leo X, organised the sale of indulgences on a vast scale, and this prompted Luther to publish his *Resolutions*. When Leo died, he went to heaven and knocked on the gate. St Peter called out and asked who it was.

'It's the Pope. Open up!'

But Peter was not satisfied.

'If you are the Pope you should have the keys to heaven like all other Popes before you.'

'I have the keys all right,' replied Leo in a plaintive voice, 'But Luther has changed the lock.'

God came down to Pakistan to see how things were going. He asked General Ayub Khan why the place was in such a mess.

Ayub replied: 'It's these no-good corrupt civilians, sir. Just get rid of them and leave the rest to me.' So God eliminated the politicos. After a while, He returned; things were even worse than before. This time he asked Yahya Khan for an explanation. Yahya blamed Ayub, his sons and their hangers-on for the troubles.

'Do the needful,' Yahya begged, 'and I'll clean the place up good and proper.'

So God's thunderbolts wiped out Ayub. On his third visit, He found a catastrophe, so he agreed with Zulfikar Ali Bhutto that democracy must return. He turned Yahya into a cockroach and swept him under a carpet; but, a few years later, he noticed the situation was still pretty awful. He went to General Zia and offered him supreme power: on one condition.

'Anything, God,' the General replied, 'You name it.'

So God said, 'Answer me one question and I'll flatten Bhutto for you like a chapati.'

Zia said: 'Fire away.'

So God whispered in his ear: 'Look, I do all these things for this country, but what I don't understand is: why don't people seem to love me any more?'

(Source: Salman Rushdie, *Shame*, Cape, London, 1983, p. 112).

---

### 5 From here to there: crossing boundaries

Brezhnev wakes up in the morning, opens the window and looks at the sun above the wall of the Kremlin. 'Hello, Leonid Illyich! Good morning to our great leader,' says the sun.

At midday, Brezhnev walks out to the balcony and the sun greets him with great affection.

'Good day to the hero of the Soviet Union, our beloved Secretary!'

In the evening, Brezhnev once more looks at the sun, but the sun is silent.

'Why don't you greet me now?' asks Brezhnev.

'You go to hell,' says the sun, 'I am in the West now.'

*Another version:*

Why does the sun have a smile on its face in the morning?

Because it knows it will be in the West in the evening.

\*　　\*　　\*

A lonely spot on the Soviet-Polish border.

Suddenly a Polish dog comes running to the border; at the same time a Soviet dog comes running towards the Polish dog. Heads down they approach each other and collide with a crash.

After a few dazed moments the Soviet dog shakes his head and asks 'What's the big hurry to get to the Soviet Union?'

'I'm hungry,' says the Polish dog. 'I want something to eat. And why are you rushing to Poland?'

'I want to bark.'

An Austrian Jew, sensing Hitler's imminent takeover of his country, is considering various options for emigration. He goes to a travel agent for advice, and the agent takes out a large globe and begins discussing the entry requirements of various countries. It soon becomes clear that many of the options are beset with difficulties. One country requires a labour permit; the second does not recognize the Austrian passport; a third has a strict money requirement for new arrivals; the fourth doesn't want any immigrants at all – least of all Jews. Finally in desperation, the Jew asks.

'Haven't you got another globe?'

A Jew is packing his suitcases after Hitler's assumption of power. His friend notices him packing a picture of Hitler.

'Why are you taking a picture of Hitler with you?' he asks, incredulously.

'To avoid nostalgia.'

Two Jews meet on the streets of New York.

'So, tell me, are you happy?'

'Sure, I'm happy. Aber glücklich bin ich nicht.'

Rabinovich was called in by the personnel department:

'Comrade Rabinovich, why did you put a lie down on your form?'

'Where?' says Rabinovich in amazement.

'Here, where it says "Do you have any relatives abroad?" you have replied "No." But you have a brother in Israel.'

'But it's me who's abroad. He's at home.'

Rabinovich, the tailor, tried to get out of the country using forged papers. When he arrived at the frontier, the passport official took his passport from him and asked:

'What's your name?'

Rabinovich blanched. He had forgotten what name he was travelling under.

'Well,' he answered, scratching his head, 'it's definately not Rabinovich.'

A Russian scientist goes to Prague to speak about the conquest of space.

'Soon,' he says, 'We'll be able to go to Mars, Jupiter, Saturn, Venus . . .'

One of his listeners timidly raises his hand.

'Please, comrade. When can we go to Vienna?'

Janos was exercising 'criticism and self-criticism' at a Party meeting in Budapest.

'A year ago,' he began, 'my four brothers and sisters, together with my mother, my father and my grandmother, deserted the fatherland and went to live in the West. They are traitors to the cause of socialist construction. That was the criticism. Now for the self-cricicism. I didn't join them.'

Two Jews are talking in Vienna in 1938.

'You know, when you think about it: we are living history – living history!'

'Personally,' says the other, 'I wouldn't mind trying geography.'

'What is the definition of a Polish string quartet?'

'A Polish orchestra just back from a Western tour.'

'Which East European sportsmen are most disappointed about the Soviet bloc's non-participation in the 1984 Olympics?'

'Those who have sold their furniture.'

'How does a clever Jew speak to a stupid Jew?'
'By telephone from Paris to Warsaw'.

---

## 6 Some national differences

A foreign tourist, with some vague knowledge of German, walks along the streets of Berlin and stops a Prussian policeman.
'Excuse me, where is Kaiser Wilhelm Strasse?'
The policeman tells him in quick-fire staccato:
'Straight ahead, turn right at the church, walk along to the third set of traffic lights, then left, then at the bookshop left again, pass the Post Office, then first left, third right, and second left again.'
The man, dazed, mutters meekly: 'Thank you.'
The policeman looks at him:
'Nicht danken. Wiederholen!' (Don't thank me. Just repeat it!)


An Israeli takes an English tourist to show him the country. He describes the country in the most colourful language and towards the end of a long day he tells his visitor:
'And you know our sense of humour is so English, we use understatement all the time?'
The visitor: 'How can you say that? You were using words such as "wonderful", "inimitable", "admirable", "matchless", etc.'
The Israeli: 'Those too were understatements.'


After the Six-Day War, two Arabs were gloomily discussing the disastrous showing of the Arab armies:
'Why do you think we did so badly? Was it because the Russian weapons were no good?'
'The weapons were fine. It was the Russian military textbooks that let us down.'
'What did they say?'

'First retreat and draw the enemy into your own territory. Then wait for the winter snows . . .'

A sociologist is doing an experiment on the behaviour of different national groups. He puts three groups, of French, English and Russians on three deserted islands to see what will happen. Each group contains two men and one woman. After six months, the sociologist goes around to see how things are turning out.

When he arrives on the island with the three English people he realizes that nothing has changed, and the three people are in fact sitting in the same place that they had been left in six months ago.

'What's the matter, why haven't you done anything?' asks the sociologist.

'Oh,' replies one of the Englishmen, 'we've been waiting for somebody to introduce us.'

The sociologist arrives on the island with the French group and finds one man working in the fields. 'Where are the others?' asks the sociologist.

'They're off making love. We split the year so each man spends six months with the woman while the other works; it's his turn now.'

When he arrives on the Russian island he finds the two men sitting drinking tea in a well-kept garden.

'Where's the woman?' asks the sociologist.

'Oh,' replies one of the Russians, 'The masses are toiling in the fields.'

The King of Norway, while in London, during the Second World War, went to the BBC to take part in a broadcast. He presented himself to the doorkeeper, explaining who he was and the programme on which he was to be interviewed. The doorkeeper telephoned the studio and said: 'There's a gentleman here who says you're expecting him. He's . . . just a minute – where did you say you was King of?'

In Heaven:
> the French do the cooking,
> the Germans do the repairs,
> the Swiss run the Government,
> the English are the policemen,
> and the Italians are the lovers.

In Hell:
> the French do the repairs,
> the Germans are the policemen,
> the English do the cooking,
> the Italians run the Government,
> and the Swiss are the lovers.


Canada could have enjoyed:
> British democracy
> French culture
> and
> American know-how

Instead it ended up with:
> British know-how
> French democracy
> and
> American culture


COMECON is based on seven fundamental principles:
> the German sense of humour,
> Polish hard work,
> Russian good-neighbourliness,
> Czech courage,
> the widespread knowledge of the Hungarian language,
> Rumanian socialist solidarity
> and Bulgarian intelligence.


The Swiss Inspector of Education goes to visit a school.
He enters a class and the teacher all excited asks:

'Who was the first man?'
Silence.
The teacher: 'Jose, tell me who was the first man?'
Jose: 'William Tell!'
Teacher: 'What about Adam?'
Jose: 'I didn't think of a foreigner.'


An Austrian officer captures a Prussian one. Haughtily, the prisoner sneers, 'We Prussians fight for our honour, but you Austrians fight only for money!'

'Why not?' retorts the Austrian. 'After all, each of us fights for what he needs most.'


Hitler dies and goes to heaven. He behaves so well there that St Peter tells him he can go back to earth again as a treat, for a week. After twenty-four hours, he's back, hammering at the pearly gates to get in.

'What's the matter, Adolf?' asks St Peter, 'You're got six more days.'

'Let me in, let me in!' cries Hitler. So St Peter unlocks the gate, lets him in and sits him down.

'Now, Adolf,' he says, 'what's the matter? Didn't you enjoy it?'

'Enjoy it?' says Hitler, 'Enjoy it? Everyone's gone mad down there since I left. I come back, and what do I find? The Jews are fighting and the Germans are making money.'


A Soviet officer is being briefed on his military mission to Cairo.

'Be polite, and don't speak out of turn. And if they tell you that Egyptian culture is older than Soviet culture, pretend to agree with them.'


Singapore in the early 1960s. In the interests of nation-building, the Government is campaigning against expatriate employees and seeking to replace them with locals. One of the Ministers is touring the General Hospital and asks a young houseman what he is doing.

'Administering a local anaesthetic.'

'Ha!' exclaimed the Minister: 'You see, we don't need those expatriates any more!'

Heard in South America after the Falkland fiasco:
'What is ego?'
'It is the Argentinian we all carry inside us.'

A Dane thinks a Swede is a German in almost human form.

Heard during the Second World War:
One Italian is a poet.
Two Italians make an opera.
Three Italians make an army in retreat.

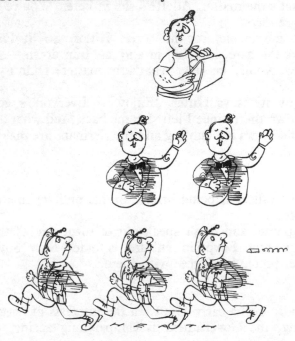

## 7 Satellites

The Soviet Union and China finally reach an agreement to reconcile their differences. But China first makes three demands.

'We need one hundred million tons of coal,' Chinese Leader Deng Xiaoping orders.

'Done,' Brezhnev replies.

'We must have twenty new cargo ships,' the Chinese leader declares.

'Agreed,' snaps Brezhnev.

'And we need a million bicycles,' the Chinese chief adds.

'Impossible,' answers Brezhnev.

The baffled Deng asks why, if Russia can provide the costly coal and ships, it can't come up with a few bikes. Brezhnev replies:

'The Poles don't make bicycles.'

A Polish schoolgirl is set an essay in which she must answer the question, 'Why do you love the Soviet Union?' She asks her father,

'Why do I love the Soviet Union?'

'Love the Soviet Union!' he shouts, 'You can't love those bloody gangsters!'

So she asks her mother,

'Why do I love the Soviet Union?'

'You can't love such a wicked country, darling,' her mother tells her.

She asks other members of her family and her friends and they all give her the same answer. So she returns to school and answers the question:

'I love the Soviet Union because no-one else does.'

Two Poles meet and congratulate each other on how well their countrymen are doing.

'Yes. We've got Brzezinski, our man in Washington. We've got John Paul, our man in Jerusalem . . .'

'Now,' says the other one, 'if we only had our man in Warsaw.'

'Why do we love the Soviet people?' asks a teacher in the German Democratic Republic.

Little Fritz raises his hand: 'Because they liberated us.'

'And why do we hate the Americans?'

'Because they didn't liberate us.'

An East German goes to consult a psychiatrist.

'Doctor,' he says, 'you must help me. My mind is completely deranged.'

'What's the trouble, my friend?'

'It's this. Every night I have the same dream. I dream I escape across the Berlin Wall!'

'Without betraying any professional secrets,' says the psychiatrist, smiling, 'I can assure you that many of your compatriots have the same dream.'

'Yes,' groans the unhappy man, 'But I dream of escaping from West to East!'

First Hungarian: 'We are lucky.'

Second Hungarian: 'Lucky? Are you crazy?'

First Hungarian: 'Just think, the Russians came as friends. Think what they would have done if they had come as enemies!'

A Hungarian peasant had come to Budapest for the first time. In a large department store he stood awe-struck in front of a massive portrait of Stalin. He turned to one of the assistants:

'Is that your boss?' he asked.

'No, that's the cashier.'

A Rumanian border-guard became friendly with his Yugoslav opposite number, and invited him back to the Rumanian sentry-post for a drink.

As he came through the door, the Yugoslav noticed a poster showing Tito licking Uncle Sam's backside, while Uncle Sam was dropping a bag of gold into Tito's outstretched hand. He began to laugh.

'But why are *you* laughing?' the Rumanian asked.

'We have a poster in our own hut of your Prime Minister licking Khruschev's backside. The only difference is that in our poster the Rumanian doesn't get any gold.'

Khruschev is visiting Nehru, whom he is trying to entice into drinking a glass of vodka. Nehru adamantly refuses, so Khruschev offers him a cement factory. Nehru still refuses, so he offers two. He refuses again, but finally and reluctantly agrees at the offer of three. Khruschev smiles broadly, so Nehru protests,

'Isn't it enough that you have humiliated me? Do you have to laugh at my humiliation?'

To which Khruschev replies:

'I was smiling at the thought of Ulbricht's face when he hears about the three cement factories.'

Soviet troops had seized the whole of Czechoslovakia and were busy arresting supporters of the overthrown regime. In desperation Dubcek consulted a Jewish soothsayer to ask his advice on what to do.

'There are two possibilities,' said the soothsayer. 'A natural one and a supernatural one.'

'What is the natural one?' asked Dubcek.

'That the archangel Gabriel will chase out the Russians with a fiery sword.'

'And the supernatural one?'

'That the Russians will decide to leave of their own accord.'

One Czech to another in Prague after the 1968 invasion.
'Czechoslovakia is the most neutral state in the world.'
'Why?'
'It doesn't even interfere in its own affairs.'

Dubcek's predecessor, Antonin Novotny, was one day called to the telephone. It was Brezhnev, phoning from Moscow.
'Yes, Comrade,' said Novotny respectfully, 'Yes, Comrade . . . yes, of course, Comrade . . . yes, yes . . . no Comrade . . . goodbye Comrade.'
Having overheard his side of the conversation, a horrified Vasil Bilak comes up to him and asks:
'Tonda, you actually said "No" to him. What did he want?'
'Nothing,' replies Novotny. 'He just asked me if I wasn't ashamed of saying "yes" all the time.'

Karel was walking through the woods near Prague when a good fairy appeared before him.
'Karel, I am your fairy godmother. I will grant you three wishes!'
Karel thought for a bit.
'I wish that the Chinese Red Army would occupy Prague and then retreat.'
The good fairy thought his wish rather strange, but said nothing.
'And your second wish?'
'I wish that the Chinese Red Army would occupy Prague and then retreat.'
'And your third wish?'
'I wish that the Chinese Red Army would occupy Prague and then retreat.'
'Your wishes will be granted,' said the fairy. 'But tell me, why do you want the Chinese Red Army to occupy Prague three times and then retreat three times?'
'Because they will have to fight their way six times across the Soviet Union.'

'Is it really true that our glorious armed forces were called in by the Czechs to defeat fascist reaction?'

'In principle, yes. The request was first made in 1939, but for technical reasons could not be positively met until 1968.'

After the launching of the first sputnik the Albanian government sends a telegram to Moscow:

'Congratulations on your great success! Entire country overcome with joy! Albania no longer smallest satellite!'

Meat is supplied jointly to the Poles by the Russians and the Czechs.

The Czechs supply the meat.

The Russians supply the coupons.

Nikita Khruschev and Nina were on their way back to Moscow by train after a state visit to the GDR. After an hour or so of travelling, Nina asked her husband if they were back in Russia yet. Nikita stuck his hand out of the window as the train pulled into a station and said:

'No, we're not back yet.'

After several more hours Nina repeated her question. Nikita once more stuck his hand out of the window and again told her that they were not yet back in Russia.

Some time later Nina asked him a third time. He stuck his hand out of the window and said:

'Yes, now we're home.'

'But how could you tell where we were just by sticking your hand out of the window?'

'Simple. The first time I stuck my hand out someone kissed it, so I knew we were still in the GDR. The second time I stuck my hand out someone spat on it, so I knew were were in Poland. The third time someone stole my wristwatch – then I knew we were back in Russia.'

The Soviet Union expresses a wish that St Vitus Cathedral, which houses the relics of St Wenceslas, be renamed St Leonid's Cathedral. The Czechs agree in principle and send a telegram to Moscow which reads: 'AGREE TO YOUR PROPOSAL. PLEASE SEND RELICS'.

A COMECON summit. The Russians place drawing pins on the chairs of the other delegations. The East Germans see the pins, sit on them and smile. The Hungarians quietly pocket theirs, sit down and howl as if in pain. The Rumanians pocket theirs, replace them with Rumanian-made pins, sit on them and smile.

Castro visits Moscow and is taken on a tour by Brezhnev. First, they go for a drink and Castro praises the beer.

'Yes, it was provided by our good friends from Czechoslovakia.'

Next, they go for a ride in a car and Castro admires the car.

'Yes, these cars are provided by our good friends from Czechoslovakia.'

They drive to an exhibition of beautiful cut glass, which Castro greatly admires. 'Yes, this glass comes from our good friends in Czechoslovakia.'

'They must be very good friends,' says Castro.

'Yes, they must,' says Brezhnev.

---

## 8 Geopolitics

Advertisement in Chilean newspaper:

SE VENDO LINDO PAIS ESQUINA CON VISTA AL MAR (FOR SALE: BEAUTIFUL CORNER COUNTRY WITH SEA VIEW)

When the new border between the Soviet Union and Finland was drawn in 1940 the proposed line ran right through the midle of a Finnish farm. The Soviet official decided to be magnanimous and suggested that they should go and ask the farmer where he wanted to live.

The Russian approached the farmer and explained to him that if the line ran on the west side of his farm he'd be a Soviet citizen and if it ran on the east side he'd be a citizen of Finland.

The farmer nodded and said that it was a very grave decision and he needed three days to think about it. After three days he came back and said:

'I wish the line to run on the east side of my farm.'

'Why?' demanded the Russian indignantly.

'You see, comrade,' replied the farmer, 'the winter in Russia is so cold.'

Nixon and Brezhnev argue about the superiority of their countries' technology.

Nixon: 'We have a computer that can tell you what

will happen in the year 1990.'

He pushes a button, and the printout says: 'Fidel Castro, President of the USA, goes to visit the Cuban territories.'

Brezhnev: 'That's nothing. Our computers can tell what is happening in the year 2000.'

He pushes a button and the printout reads: 'All quiet on the Chinese-Finnish border.'


Hitler and Stalin in a cloud, drift over Prague as tanks roll into the city from the USSR and the GDR.

'My dear Joseph,' says Hitler, 'why *did* we fight one another?'


Question to Radio Erevan:

'Is there a real chance of friendship with the Germans?'

'Basically yes. They seem to have forgiven us for their attack on the Soviet Union.'


The Danube Conference:

Hungary and the Soviet Union reach agreement on the following points: the Soviet Union may navigate the Danube lengthwise, the Hungarians breadthwise.


Before Chairman Mao died, one of his aides went rushing into the Chairman's office.

'Chairman Mao! Chairman Mao! Bad News! Bulgaria has declared war on China.'

Mao stared at him, then asked:

'And in which hotel do they stay?'


Mintoff, the Prime Minister of Malta, complains to Brezhnev about Soviet unco-operativeness in trade and other matters. Finding no response, he gives an ultimatum:

'Either you help us or we'll declare war on you.'
'Is that wise, given your size and position in the world?' asks Brezhnev. Mintoff is indignant:
'We have our Bofors guns and an army of eight hundred men.'
Brezhnev again counsels caution, and Mintoff hesitates.
'Ah, you are beginning to see reason,' says Brezhnev.
'I was wondering,' says Mintoff, 'where we could put all the Russian prisoners of war.'

Definition of an Argentinian:
'A Uruguayan with visions of grandeur.'

An Israeli and a European diplomat are involved in a heated argument about the UN. Finally, the Israeli gets exasperated and says:
'Well, you should know that there are four sides to every question.'
'Four sides?' asks the diplomat.
'Yes,' replies the Israeli. 'My side, your side, the right side and the UN side.'

Two jokes popular before the war in Lebanon:

An Englishman, an American and an Israeli are captured by cannibals, and while the cauldron is warming up, each is to be granted a final wish. The Englishman asks for a cup of tea, the American for a hot dog, and their wishes are granted. The Israeli then makes his request – that the cannibal chief kick him up the backside. The wish fulfilled, the Israeli pulls his Uzi submachine gun from under his shirt, kills his captors and sets his companions free.
'But why did you ask him to kick you?' they ask.
'Because otherwise I would be accused of aggression.'

Two Israelis argue about ways and means of getting

American support.

First: 'It's very simple. We declare a war on the USA, we lose and then we get all the American aid we need.'

Second: 'But what if we win?'

On the other side of the moon, the Russian and American astronauts meet.

'At last!' they say in German, 'We can speak our own mother-tongue.'

A Unionist candidate in Belfast thought it might be a good idea to stress his connections with England.

'I was born an Englishman, I live like an Englishman, and I shall die an Englishman.'

A voice from the back of the hall:

'Sir, have ye no ambition at all?'

Three Israelis sit in a coffee house lamenting he economic crisis.

First: 'If only we had some oil.'

Second: 'If only Moses had taken us to Saudi Arabia.'

Third: 'Only then they would have found oil in Canaan.'

A scorpion having crossed most of the Sahara on his way towards Mecca found himself on the banks of the Suez Canal. It was an impossible barrier and it seemed he would never achieve his goal.

The scorpion came upon a frog basking just offshore and asked the frog to ferry him across the canal.

The frog replied, 'No, you are a scorpion and would sting me to death.'

The scorpion protested: 'That is ridiculous. You would die and I would drown. Please help me.'

'All right,' said the frog. 'Climb on my back.'

In the middle of the canal, the scorpion stung the frog.

'Why,' asked the frog as they are about to drown, 'did you do that?'

'Because,' said the scorpion, 'this is the Middle East.'

---

## 9 Identities

A Jew comes to an inn very late at night and is forced to share a room with a Russian officer. Not wanting to meet him he asks the innkeeper to wake him up very early in the morning because he has to catch the first train. The Jew undresses and goes to bed and he is awakened by the innkeeper when it is still dark outside. He dresses quickly and goes out and to his surprise all the soldiers salute him. When he mounts the train he look at the mirror and realizes that he is wearing uniform.

'Damn the innkeeper,' cries the Jew, 'he woke up the wrong man!'

A Jew was forced to flee his old homeland, and go to Israel.

'Dear God,' he sighed, 'two thousand years we pray in vain to return – and now it has to happen to me!'

Chaim and Abe meet after a long separation.

'Ah!' cries Abe, 'How are you? How is your family? How are your children? I remember, you had three sons. They must be grown up?'

'Yes,' says Chaim, 'they are. One lives in Moscow, he's building Communism. The second lives in Warsaw, he too is building Communism. The other one lives in Israel.'

'Is he building Communism too?'

'Are you out of your mind? In his own country?'

It was decided in the late 1960s to get rid of a Jewish

member of the Polish politburo. So he was sent to sell Polish cars to the Germans. After two weeks he returned with a contract. Surprised but determined, his colleagues sent him to the United States to sell Polish computers. After a month he returned with a string of orders. Amazed, but now adamant, they despatched him to the People's Republic of China to sell Polish rice to the Chinese. Months passed and it seemed that he was at last disposed of. After six months, however, he returned with a signed contract.

'But how did you manage it?' they asked.

'It was difficult.' he admitted, 'It took me six months to find another Jew.'

Rabinowich applies for membership to the Communist party, and he is required to answer a few questions.

'Who was Karl Marx?'

'I don't know,' replies Rabinovich.

'Lenin?'

'Never heard of him!'

'Are you playing games with me?' asks the official.

'Not at all,' says Rabinovich. 'Do you know Herschel Solzberg?'

'No,' says the official.

'What about Yankel Horowitz?'

'Never heard of him!'

'Nahum Davidowich?'

'No.'

'Well,' says Rabinowich. 'That's the way it goes. You've got your friends and I've got mine.'

After the outbreak of the First World War in 1914, a young woman accosts a Cambridge don in the street.

'And what are you doing to defend Civilization?' she demands.

'Madam,' he replies, 'I *am* the Civilization that is being defended.'

A poor girl from the East End of London was invited to a charity tea at the home of a local magistrate's wife.

The little girl sat down at the table, turned to her hostess and said: 'I see you keep your house very clean. Cleanliness is next to godliness, you know.'

The lady smiled, and gave her husband a knowing look.

'Is your husband working?' asked the little girl.

'But of course!' said the lady. 'What a strange question for you to ask.'

'And are you both keeping off the drink?'

'What an impertinent little girl!' cried the magistrate's wife. 'When you are out visiting you should take care to behave like a lady, my child.'

'But I do!' said the little girl. 'When the ladies visit our house they always ask these questions.'

An earnest and wealthy English socialist was forced to travel by train for the first time in many years when his

Rolls was involved in a collision. However, he welcomed this chance to have some contact with 'ordinary people'. As he passed through the station he said to the man who punched his ticket: 'How long have you been doing this?'
'Oh,' said the ticket man, 'nearly twenty years.'
The traveller studied his ticket carefully.
'You do it very well,' he said appreciatively.

The millionaire MP was called on by a member of the BBC television staff who asked him to appear in a programme. When all other details were settled the BBC man asked 'Will a £50 fee for a half-hour programme be all right?'
'Certainly,' said the MP, 'just hold on a minute and I'll give you a cheque.'

Nehru arrived in Moscow on an official visit. It was 7 a.m. He went out on the balcony of his official residence. In the street below he could see trams and buses jammed full of people.
'Who are they all?' asked Nehru.
'Russia's masters,' replied Khruschev.
11 a.m. Nehru went out on the balcony again. He saw a number of black limousines driving by.
'Who are they?' asked Nehru.
'That's us,' announced Khruschev proudly. 'The servants of the people!'

Mao, Brezhnev and Dubcek on an international flight. A stewardess prepares to make an announcement:
'Ladies and gentlemen, we are extremely fortunate. We have Jesus Christ on board. He is about to come into the cabin and grant each passenger one wish.'
Christ enters the cabin and walks up to Mao.
'What's your wish?' Christ asks him.
'I wish that all the Soviet Revisionists would disappear

from the face of the earth,' says Mao.

'Very well,' says Christ and proceeds to Brezhnev.

'What is your wish?' Jesus asks him.

'I wish that all these Chinese Deviationists would disappear,' says Brezhnev.

'Very well,' says Jesus, and moves on to Dubcek.

'And what is your wish?' asks Jesus.

'Comrade Jesus,' says Dubcek, 'are your really going to do everything these two asked you?'

'Of course,' replies Jesus, 'I'm God.'

'Mm . . .' says Dubcek, 'in that case, I'll settle for a cup of coffee.'


Bashir Gemayel, the murdered Christian President of Lebanon, arrives in Heaven:

Jesus is sent to interview him.

'What did you do in your lifetime?' Jesus asks.

Silence.

'I must know,' pleads Jesus, but Gemayel remains obstinately silent.

An angel is sent for to find out what is going on and asks Gemayel why he is not answering Jesus's questions.

'Why should I?' replies Gemayel, 'I don't talk to Palestinians.'


The Pope died, but was allowed to return to earth for a day to speak to the Cardinals. They gathered round him eagerly.

'What's He like?' they clamoured. 'Is He very old with a long white beard like in all the paintings? Tell us! Describe Him!'

'Well,' the Pope began, 'to start with, She's black.'


Kaiser Joseph II loved to mingle with his people in the market place.

One day he asks for the price of two eggs.

'Two guilders,' replies the seller.

'You are crazy, are those eggs so rare?'
'Not the eggs,' replies the seller, 'The Kaisers.'


During the Pope's visit to Poland, General Jaruzelski telephones the Pontiff.
'I have a request to make, Your Holiness. Might I travel with you tomorrow in your pope-mobile?'
'Yes, my son,' said the Pope, 'but why?'
'I just wanted to see what it's like to be cheered by the Polish people.'

# 3 *Debunking and Unmasking*

*Kundera, the Czech writer, suggests that tragedy may create an aura of greatness, while those who have known the comedies of life have no such illusions. Is this why humour in general and jokes in particular are so attractive to those who try to deflate illusions of grandeur? Is this why political figures and institutions are so frequently the butt of jokes? The jokes in this section are uniformly deflationary, puncturing pomposity and pretensions to underserved deference and all types of authority. They strip away veils, but they do not reveal anything hidden, surprising or previously unknown. Reassuringly, they portray the veils as transparent and tawdry.*

*Unmasking and debunking are the two most piously observed commandments in joking. Here the pleasures of sweet revenge show clearly. Note, however, that some of the jokes in the following part could equally have been listed here, mixing, as they do, unmasking with quiescence and debunking with despair.*

## 1 The powerful

'Have you heard the story about Brezhnev's death?'

'No, how does it go?'

'I don't know the details, but it seems to start beautifully . . .'

During the dictatorship Papadopoulos and Paddakos are being driven around the countryside in a limousine, which suddenly strikes a pig that was crossing the road, and kills it.

Papadopoulos tells the driver to go to the nearby farmhouse and to pay the owners for the loss of their pig.

The driver walks into the farmhouse with his wallet in his hand and after a while returns to the car, bearing gifts of cheese, wine and olives.

'What happened?' they ask him.

'I don't know. I just said, "Zito Papadopoulos! The Pig is dead!" and they gave me all this.'

A man ran through the steets of Moscow shouting: 'Khruschev is a swine!'

He was seized and given twenty-one years: one year for defamation and 20 years for leaking state secrets.

Pakistan's leader, General Zia, goes to the barber for a haircut. Every now and then the barber asks him, 'When will you have elections?'

First he replies 'When the time is ripe.'

Then he explains about problems on the borders.

Every time the question is asked, he gives another reason.

Eventually, Zia asks angrily: 'Why are you so interested in the elections?'

'Oh I'm not,' says the barber. 'It's just that every time I mention elections your hair stands on end.'

*Another version:*

The barber says to Brezhnev: 'It's just professional interest – every time I mention Poland your hair stands on end.'

\*   \*   \*

One afternoon, Khruschev disguised his appearance and went to see a film in a Moscow suburban cinema. After the feature film there was a short newsreel. A picture of

Khruschev appeared on the screen. Everyone stood up, except for Khruschev himself. He sat there with tears in his eyes, deeply moved by this spontaneous show of popular affection.

A man tapped him on the shoulder and whispered:

'Get up, you fool! We all think the way you do, but what's the point of sticking your neck out?'

De Gaulle slips on the wet floor, coming from his bath.

'Mon Dieu!' exclaims his wife.

The General gets up slowly from the floor and says: 'How many times do I have to tell you that at home you may call me by my first name.'

(French version: 'Ma chérie! Tu m'as reconnu.')

A man in a queue outside a butcher's shop in Warsaw gets furious:

'I've had enough of this standing and waiting. I'm going off to murder Gomulka.'

Two hours later he returns, looking glum.

'No good,' he says. 'There was a queue.'

The two leaders of the Greek dictatorship, Papadopoulos and Paddakos, are together at Headquarters when the Governor of Korydallos, the largest prison in Greece, comes to see them.

'The prisoners have several grievances, and they are threatening to go on hunger strike unless their demands are met.'

'What do they want?' asks Papadopoulos.

'They want to see their wives once a week for sex.'

Papadopoulos agrees. Paddakos is shocked at his leniency.

A week later the Governor returns: 'There is more trouble at the prison. The prisoners now want television in their cells and they say they'll go on strike if the demand is not met.'

Papadopoulos again agrees. Paddakos is appalled but again says nothing.

After a month the Governor again visits Headquarters.

'The prisoners now demand weekends off for good behaviour just like they have in Denmark.'

Papadopoulos agrees but Paddakos can no longer keep silent.

'Why are you so generous to these prisoners? We should be generous to our schools, not to our prisons.'

'Look,' Papadopoulos replies, 'When we finish up here, we won't be going to school.'

A journalist, waiting for hours in the German President Hindenburg's ante-room to be admitted for an interview, gets so hungry that he unpacks his sandwiches. Meissner, Hindenburg's Secretary of State, discovers the journalist munching away, with the paper wrapping lying on the table. 'For God's sake,' cries Meissner, 'get rid of that! If the old man finds a piece of paper lying around he'll sign it.'

An American biographer of Lenin is looking for details about his life in London and so she goes to the library at the British Museum. They put her in touch with an ancient ex-door keeper who was working there at the time that Lenin studied there.

'Do you remember Lenin?' she asks.

'Never heard of him,' he says.

She presses him, but he insists, claiming to have known all his regular readers. Finally, she has a brainwave:

'What about Ulyanov?'

'Oh, *him*! Of course, I remember him. Funny bloke. Whatever became of him?'

Harold Wilson is told by his Private Secretary that two

visitors are waiting to see him.

'Who are they?' demands Wilson.

'The Archbishop of Canterbury and the Director of the Confederation of British Industry.'

'Show the Archbishop in first,' Wilson says, 'I only have to kiss his hand.'

When the Troubles first began, Paisley made enquiries about a plot in the local cemetery. The clerk told him:

'The price is £100. That may sound a lot, but you won't be disturbed for two hundred years.' Paisley made some rapid calculations on the back of an envelope.

'I'll give you half a penny. After all, I'll only need it for three days.'

President Reagan woke up in the middle of the night, seized with doubts about his policies. Consumed by

uncertainty, he decided to take a stroll on the streets of the Capital. Finding himself at the Washington Memorial, he called out:
'What should I do?'
A voice from deep within the Memorial replied,
'Go to the Congress.'
A little further on, Reagan found himself at the Jefferson Memorial. Again he cried out,
'What should I do?'
'Go to the people,' replied the voice.
Still troubled, Reagan continued walking untill he reached the Lincoln Memorial. Once more he asked the question,
'What should I do?'
The reply came instantly from deep within the Memorial:
'Go to the theatre.'


Two little twin boys are sent home from school with a note saying,
'Dear Mrs. Smith, your boys say their names are Nixon and Agnew. Is this true or are they making fun of me?'
Mrs Smith writes back:
'Dear teacher, the name is Miss Smith, not Mrs Smith, and if you had two little bastards, what would you call them?'


Ben Gurion, Golda Meir and Begin meet in Hell and discuss their situation.
Ben Gurion says:
'I was the founder of the State of Israel, but I insulted a great number of people and you can see what happened.'
Golda Meir says:
'I was the Prime Minister in very difficult times and I saved the country from great dangers, but I was too stubborn and too righteous and . . . here I am.'

Begin remains silent and the other two turn to him:
'Why are you in Hell?'
Begin says:
'I am Menachem Begin, son of Hasia, pupil of
Jabotinsky, Prime Minister of Israel, this place is not
Hell and I am not here.'


In 1945, de Gaulle receives General de Lattre de
Tassigny, who declares:
'France thinks that . . .'
De Gaulle interrupts drily:
'When I want to know what France thinks, I will ask
myself.'


On De Gaulle's retirement from politics, Couve de
Murville spoke tactfully to the General:
'Mon Général, I would like to ask you a question. In
the event, obviously improbable as it is, that death
should visit you one day, would it be indiscreet to ask
you where you would like to be buried? Doubtless, next
to Napoleon at the Invalides?'
De Gaulle is furious, 'What? Next to that junior
officer?'
'Perhaps at the Arc de Triomphe, then, mon
Général?'
'So that American tourists can come and desecrate my
tomb? Never!'
'Then I have a solution,' says Couve, 'Beside the
Maid of Orleans.'
'Now that's a good idea,' the General replies. 'After
all, she merits it.'


General Zia goes to a military hospital for a check-up,
and notices a pretty nurse, who is wearing a foreign-
made uniform.
'Your uniform is nice,' he says, 'but I say 'Be
Pakistani and buy Pakistani.'

So the nurse tears off her uniform.

'My dear,' says Zia, 'I see your underwear is Marks and Spencers.' So she tears these off.

'Now,' says Zia to her, 'Let us embrace Islam.'

Mao's famous swim in the Yangtze. As he reaches the river bank, the onlookers duly cheer and congratulate him.

'Just a moment,' he says, 'what I want to know first is who pushed me in!'

President Nasser was walking on the banks of the Nile one day when he hears a ghostly voice:

'A-Rais, please bring me a horse, a horse.'

The next day the same thing happened.

Nasser decides to report it to General Amer.

The two of them go down to the Nile and they hear a voice:

'You fool. I demanded a horse and you've brought me an ass!'

Assad and his brother are flying over Syria. Assad takes some money and throws it out of the window:
'At least one of my citizens will be happy.'
His brother throws more money.
'More citizens will be happy.'
The pilot comes over and throws both of them out of the window:
'Now all our citizens are happy!'


A reception is held in Paris. One of the guests, President Numeiri of the Sudan, loses his invitation. He arrives and explains who he is to the guard at the door.
'But how do I know who you are?' asks the guard, 'An hour ago, Pablo Picasso came without his invitation, I have him a brush and he painted a marvellous painting. And half an hour ago, Pablo Casals came without his invitation, I gave him a cello, and he played beautiful music . . .'
'Who is this Pablo Picasso and Pablo Casals?'
'Say no more,' says the guard, 'You're President Numeiri.'


The Shah of Iran was having trouble keeping his workers in line, so he thought he might invest in a few dozen extra tanks. Consequently he visited an arms factory in Coventry. He had just met the managing director when the lunchtime hooter sounded. To the Shah's horror, hundreds of workers downed tools and rushed out of the factory.
'We must escape!' cried the Shah. 'The workers have risen. We will have to capture one of your tanks and fight our way to safety.'
'It's nothing to worry about,' the managing director assured him. 'It happens every day. In half an hour's time, another hooter will sound and they'll all rush back in again.'
'Really?' the Shah replied. 'In that case, forget the tanks – I'll take a thousand hooters instead.'

Gomulka decides to send a research team to England to discover why the accident rate is so much lower on English than Polish roads. The investigators conclude that this is so because in England, drivers drive on the left. So, as a pilot experiment, 10 per cent of Polish drivers are ordered to drive on the left.

'Have you heard that General Pinochet of Chile is to receive the Nobel Prize for mathematics?'
'For *mathematics*! Why?'
'He can get a square head into a round cap,'

Brezhnev and Kosygin were on their way back to Moscow after a Warsaw Pact meeting.
'Did you see that marvellous wrist-watch de Gaulle gave Ceaucescu?' asked Brezhnev.
'No,' said Kosygin, 'show it to me.'

Indira Gandhi dies and tries to enter paradise. She knocks on the Gate and after a long time an angel opens the door and says: 'Sorry, Mrs Gandhi, wrong floor: please go down the stairs.'
After a short while, Mrs. Gandhi is again knocking furiously on the same gate, shouting, 'Let me in, let me in!'
'What is it now?' asks the angel politely.
'I demand political asylum!'

Franco, reflecting on his longevity:
'The terrible thing about keeping pets is that they do not last long. I once had a tortoise and was very fond of it, but it grew old and died.'

Franco lies dying. A crowd gathers outside his house and prays for him.

Franco: 'What are those people doing there?'
Doctor: 'General, they have come to bid farewell.'
Franco: 'Why, where are they going?'


A man came into a pub in Co. Kildare, mumbling and swearing over and over,
'De Valera has a face like a horse's arse.'
There was something of a stir among the locals. At the third or fourth repetition of this imprecation, they moved up on him.
'Look here,' they tell him, 'you can't say that sort of thing in here.'
The man is somewhat non-plussed, 'I know I might have gone a bit far,' he says, 'but I didn't realize that this was De Valera country.'
'It isn't,' they say, 'it's good horse-breeding country.'


In 1976 Kissinger went to China and he went to a tailor to have a suit custom-made. But the tailor told him:
'I'm sorry, we can't make you a suit because you're such a big man that we don't have enough cloth of the same type and colour for you.'
So Kissinger went to Spain and again tried to have a tailor-made suit, but again the tailor told him that, since he was such a big man, they didn't have enough cloth.
So Kissinger tried in London, and in Paris, and in Africa, but always he received the same reply.
Finally, he went to Israel and went to a tailor for a suit.
'Oh yes, for *you*, Mr. Kissinger, we can make two suits!'


*Another version*:

Mr. Mintoff buys a length of cloth and goes to a tailor in the south of Malta (where he is most popular) to have it made up into a suit.
'Only enough cloth here for a jacket,' says the tailor.
As he travels elsewhere in the South, he gets the same

answer from other tailors. Finally he goes to a tailor in Sliema in the heartland of the opposition party, who makes him a fine suit with a waistcoat too.

'How did you do it?' he asks.

'Listen,' says the tailor, 'you not such a big man here.'

\*    \*    \*

There are six people on an aircraft: the pilot, Brezhnev, Carter, Giscard, a priest and a young man. When something goes wrong with the plane, the pilot announces that he is taking one of the five parachutes, and that they must decide between themselves who will take the remaining four.

Brezhnev declares that since he is the only hope for the spread of Communism he must jump and taking a parachute jumps out of the plane.

Carter declares that he is the only hope for defence of the Free World against the spread of Communism, and he too takes a parachute and jumps.

Then Giscard gets up: 'I am the leader of the French nation and the most intelligent of world leaders. I must jump,' and he too jumps out of the plane.

Then the priest rises and says to the young man – 'My son, I am old and have lived my time, take the last parachute and jump.'

But the young man protests: 'Father, hurry up – there are two parachutes left, one for each of us. Put on one of them and jump.'

'But how is that?' asks the priest.

'That guy who said he is the most intelligent world leader – he took my sleeping-bag.'

At the time when the campaign for full employment dominated official publicity, it was asked why Hitler always pressed his peaked cap against his abdomen when reviewing march-pasts. 'He's protecting Germany's last unemployed.'

Sent to Rome for delicate negotiations with the Holy See, Goering wires Hitler: 'MISSION ACCOMPLISHED. POPE UNFROCKED. TIARA AND PONTIFICAL VESTMENTS A PERFECT FIT.'

Goering's aide de camp runs into his boss's room:
'A burst water-pipe is flooding the air-force ministry, Sir!'
Goering springs to his feet: 'Quick! Hand me my Admiral's uniform!'

At night Emmy Goering wakes up and sees her naked husband with his back to her perform a weird ritual with his marshal's baton. Challenged by her, he explains: 'I am promoting my underpants to overpants.'

A Berliner and a Viennese exhange air-raid reminiscences. The former says: 'The raid was so heavy that for hours after the all-clear, window panes were hurtling down into the streets.' 'That's nothing,' says the other, 'In Vienna after the raid, portraits of the Führer were raining down into the streets for days.'

It will be peace when Franco's widow stands before the open grave of Mussolini and asks 'Who shot Hitler?'

At a Cabinet meeting, Fidel announced that Felipe Pazos had resigned as President of the Central Bank. Castro asked:
'Since we need someone to replace Felipe, which of you is an *economista*?'
Che Guevara raised his hand and Fidel replied:
'OK, Che, you're the next President of the Bank.'
After the meeting, Fidel went up to Che and said:
'Che, I didn't know you were an *economista*.'

'Oh my God,' said Che, 'I thought you said *Communista.*'

It is known that in 1968 there was an assassination attempt on the life of the Party's First Secretary, Comrade Leonid Ilyich Brezhnev. It is also known that a certain Lieutenant Popov fired a shot intended for the First Secretary but succeeded in wounding only Brezhnev's chauffeur. Political historians are still disputing the facts surrounding this incident. One group maintains that Lieutenant Popov's aim was thrown off balance by certain persons in the crowd grabbing for his pistol, shouting 'Give it to me! Let me do it!' Another school of thought familiar with this near-tragic event asserts that the chauffeur was wounded after the bullet ricocheted off Brezhnev's head.

Under the Austro-Hungarian Empire, the Emperor often borrowed money from private bankers. Franz Josef was hoping to fix up a loan with a certain Jewish banker who went to the Schönbrunn Palace for an audience.

While waiting in the ante-room, he was engaged in conversation by the Minister of the Interior, who said to him: 'Herr Rosenthal, the Emperor is very worried by the activities of your son, Moritz. He has been too much involved with all these socialist groups. As you must know, Herr Rosenthal, that is very dangerous.

After some more of this, the Jewish banker got up and made for the door. The Minister, looking surprised, said: 'But, Herr Rosenthal, what about your audience with the Emperor?'

'Look,' said the banker, 'There's no point. If he is afraid of my boy, Moritz, how can I trust him?'

Heard in Moscow before Gorbachev's days:

'What is the difference between Andropov and Chernenko?'

'Body temperature.'

Mrs Thatcher has died and her coffin is being carried to the graveside by eight men. Suddenly, the lid opens and her head appears.

'Four men are enough for this job,' she intones, 'if our standard of dying is to be maintained.'

'Listen Maggie,' says one of them, 'The country has carried you and your mad ideas for twenty years, so we can carry you for a few more minutes. Let's not make a task of a pleasure.'

'Did you hear that Denis Thatcher has died?'

'No! What were his last words?'

'He didn't have any. She was with him to the end.'

Margaret Thatcher can't understand the continuing strife in the Middle East. She thinks the Arabs and the Jews should live in peace like good Christians.

A toast to Mrs Thatcher, the Iron Lady: 'May she rust in peace!'

Press Secretary Bill Moyers was saying Grace at breakfast once when President Lyndon Johnson bellowed,
'Speak up Bill, I can't hear a damn thing.'
Moyers looked up and said quietly,
'I wasn't addressing you, Mr President.'

The King told his clown: 'Do something to shock me and then I want you to find an excuse that shocks me even more!'
After a few days, the King stands by the window looking out on his beautiful garden.
The clown comes over and pinches the King's behind.
'What do you think you are doing?' shouts the king.
'I'm sorry, please excuse me,' says the clown, 'I thought it was the Queen.'

General Westmoreland: 'What can we give Eisenhower for his birthday?'
General Patten: 'A book perhaps?'
General Westmoreland: 'Naw, he's got one of those already.'

In Tunis a man goes to the newstand every morning to read the front page of the daily papers. But he never buys one. At last, the newsagent loses his temper:
'You'll have to buy the papers if you want to read them.'

The man, somewhat embarrassed, tries to excuse himself:

'Yes, but you know, I'm interested in reading the obituaries, nothing else.'

'All the more reason why you should buy the papers. The obituaries are on the inside pages. But I've noticed you only read the front page every time.'

'Yes, but you see, what I'm waiting for will be on the front page.'

---

## 2 Bureaucracy

When the manager of a collective farm took office he found two letters in his desk. They were from his predecessor and with them was an instruction to keep them safe and open them when he got into difficulties.

Some years later the farm failed to meet its quota, the manager remembered the letters and opened the first one. It said:

'Blame everything on me.'

This advice proved successful, and for a while his position was secure. But then the grain harvest failed and the going got rough again. The manager opened the second letter. It said:

'Prepare two letters.'

A Soviet guerrilla is being sent behind enemy lines. He is given a brief to board a certain aeroplane that will take him to point M. There he is to jump. His parachute will open and when he lands he will find a car waiting to take him where he is to go. The plane reaches point M and the guerrilla jumps. He pulls the ring on his parachute but nothing happens. He tries the reserve parachute. Again nothing. 'As usual!' he complains. 'Wherever you go, the same old Soviet foul-ups. I bet the car won't even be waiting when I arrive!'

'Why do Bulgarian militiamen walk in threes?'

'Because one knows how to read, the second how to write and the third is there to keep an eye on these two dangerous intellectuals.'

By special favour, a Soviet worker who is leaving to spend three weeks' holiday by the Black Sea, has obtained a permit authorizing him to get his train ticket without having to queue. He arrives at the station and shows his ticket to an employee. 'Fine,' says the latter, pointing to a vast queue, 'Go to the end and wait. That's the queue for people who have special permission not to queue.'

A newcomer to hell is confronted by two doors with bold inscriptions over them:

'Socialist Hell.'

'Capitalist Hell.'

'Excuse me,' he asks his accompanying guard, 'What's the difference?'

'In the Socialist Hell you are boiled and flogged: in the Capitalist Hell it is the other way around.'

'So, which is the better place to go?' asks the newcomer nervously.

'The Socialist Hell, of course.'

'But it seems to me that there is practically no difference between them.'

'Well, in the Socialist Hell there is always a shortage of coal, or labour, or both . . .'

A foreign tourist on holiday in Spain goes to the administrative offices at 4 p.m. to find the door closed.

Finding a concierge, he enquires:

'Do Spanish civil servants not work in the afternoon?'

'In fact,' replies the concierge, 'It's the morning they don't work. The afternoons they spend at home.'

During the economic recession in Israel in the fifties, it was forbidden to bring into the country goods from abroad, particularly coffee. One day a man arrives at Haifa port carrying a sack on his shoulders. He is stopped by the customs official:

'What is it that you have in your sack?'

'Oh,' replies the man, 'this is food for birds!'

The official becomes suspicious and orders him to open the sack. He looks inside and sure enough it is coffee!

'Food for birds!' says the official mockingly. 'Have you ever heard of birds eating coffee?'

'Well,' says the man, 'if they want to they will and if they don't they won't.'

A Berliner, whose flat was totally destroyed in the course of an air-raid on the German capital, went to his local reparations office to seek compensation.

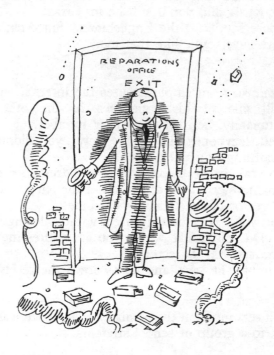

In the foyer were two doors, one for those who had suffered serious damage and one for those who had only suffered light damage. Since he had lost everything, he went through the first door.

At the end of a corridor he came across two doors, one for the well-to-do, another for those in need. Since he was absolutely penniless, he went through the second door.

Once again he came to two more doors: one for members of the Party, and one for non-members. Since he was not a Nazi, he opened the door for non-members – and found himself out on the pavement again.

During the Attlee Government there was a story about an American from Texas who was trying to impress his English hosts by the size of his home state.

'You know,' he said, 'You can board the train in Dallas, Texas and you can travel for twenty-four hours continuously and you'll still be in Texas.

'I dare say,' said the Englishman. 'Since nationalisation we have trains like that too.'

In a ministry, an employee uses the internal telephone to call one of his colleagues in the office. But unfortunately, he dials the wrong number.

'Well, lazybones,' he begins gaily, 'you didn't arrive this morning until 10 o'clock!'

'Do you realise whom you are addressing?' says an indignant voice on the other end of the telephone. 'I am the Director of the Minister's Cabinet.'

'And you!' says the employee, without losing his *sang froid*. 'Do you realize whom you are addressing?'

'No,' says the Director.

'Humph,' he says, and slams down the receiver.

A civil servant from the Ministry of Defence was giving a talk to a group of school students.

'What would you do if there was a nuclear attack?'
one pupil asked.

'Well, I'd cover myself in a shroud, and proceed
slowly towards the cemetery.'

'Why *slowly*?'

'To avoid causing a panic.'

A Minister made the mistake of ticking off a civil
servant who wrote the speeches on which his reputation
was largely based. At the next speech, after the
introductory witticisms in the first two pages, he turned
to page 3 and read: 'Now, old chap, you're on your
own.'

A writer from the Chechen Autonomous Republic in the
North Caucasus visits Moscow to meet officials of the
Russian Republic Writers Union.

'And what do you think of our great Tolstoy?' they
ask him.

'I don't think I've heard of him.'

'Well, what about our incomparable Dostoevsky?'

'Never read him. I'm afraid.'

'Then what about the inestimable Chekov?'

'Never heard of him.'

The Russian writers are beyond exasperation: 'What
do you mean by coming all this way to see us and then
wasting our time like this. You haven't even bothered to
read any of our great Russian writers!'

'I am very sorry,' says the Chechen writer, 'I am a
Chechen writer, not a Chechen reader.'

When his son Titus criticized him for imposing a tax on
urinals, the Emperor Vespasian held up to his son's
nose a coin from the first tax collection, asking,

'So, do you dislike the smell?'

The son said: 'No.'

Vespasian replied, 'Well, it's from the piss.'

# 3 Parties and elections

Hungary's Interior Minister calls the Head of State.
'Thieves have broken into the Ministry this evening.'
'Have they stolen something?'
'Alas, yes. All the results of the next elections.'

In Poland, a Party secretary asks the local priest if he can borrow the pews from the church for the next Congress. The priest refuses, pointing out that the last time he lent them they came back all dirty.

The secretary says: 'If you don't lend me the pews, I won't let the Young Pioneers help with the Mass.'

The priest says: 'In that case, I'm not going to marry any more young Communists.'

The secretary says, 'In that case, I won't allow the Workers' Guard to join the Procession.'

The priest says: 'In that case, I'm not going to write your November 7 speeches anymore.'

The secretary says: 'In that case, I won't come to Mass any more.'

The priest says: 'In that case, I shall leave the Party.'

In 1938 a rigged 'people's plebiscite' was held in Nazi Germany. 'Isn't it amazing,' said Tunnes, '98 per cent voted for Hitler.'

'It certainly is,' replied Schall. 'And what's really amazing is that I keep meeting the 2 per cent.'

In the 1955 elections, Mapai was the dominant party in Israel. On entering the polling station in a remote village of new immigrants each elector is handed a sealed envelope by a Mapai party official. He then is told to go into the polling booth, stay there for a while and then come out and place the same envelope into the ballot box. Everybody obeys but one man begins to open his envelope on his way to the booth. The party official dashes up to him:

'What do you think you are doing, you fool?'

'I want to see what I am voting for.'

'But don't you know that in Israel we have a secret ballot?'


A little Protestant boy in East Belfast was standing in the street, crying his eyes out. A lady stopped to console him.

'What's the matter, little boy?'

Between sobs, the child replied:

'My father doesn't love me.'

'Of course he does,' she tried to reassure him, 'What makes you say such a thing?'

'He's been back to vote three times since he died, but he's never come to see me once.'

*Another version:*

Two fellows went to a graveyard just before a Texan election and began copying down the names on the tombstones. Up and down the rows they went getting names until they came to a tombstone so old and worn that it was hard to decipher the name on it. One of them wanted to skip it, but the other tried to read the inscription.

'What is the matter with you?' cried the impatient one. 'Why are you standing here?'

'Well, Ah care,' said the second fellow. 'This man's got every bit as much right to vote as all the rest of all these fellows here.'

\*    \*    \*

One of the witnesses at a commission enquiring into a case of alleged bribery stated that he had received £25 to vote for the British Conservative Party. On cross-examination it was revealed that he had also received £25 to vote Labour. The chairman of the commission then asked the witness:

'For whom did you actually vote?'
The witness replied: 'I voted, sir, according to my conscience.'

In 1967, President Johnson and Vice-President Humphrey went to Chicago to discuss an extremely important matter with Mayor Daley. For security reasons, they decided to take a rowing-boat to the middle of Lake Michigan and talk about it there.

Some distance from the shore, the boat began to leak. So much water seeped in that they decided the boat could hold only one. They held a secret ballot to find out who would stay on board. Mayor Daley won by three votes to two.

Two Americans are talking.
'You know that I'm standing in the elections for the post of State Governor. I hope I can count on your vote?'
'No,' says the other. 'I'm sorry, but it is impossible.'
'But why?'
'Because I'm a Democrat.'
'And why are you a Democrat?'
'Well, my great-grandfather was a Democrat, my grandfather was a Democrat, my father was a Democrat, so I'm a Democrat.'
'But look here,' says the first, 'if your great-grandfather was an idiot, your grandfather was an idiot, and your father was an idiot, would you then be an idiot?'

Chairman of a Welsh education committee:
'Right lads, we'll now take a vote. All those in favour say "aye" and all those against say "I resign".'

'Why does a Labour government always resemble a violin?'
'Because it's held on the left and played on the right.'

Conservative election agent to canvassers:
'What I want you to do is to go and knock on people's doors in the middle of their favourite television programme. Then tell them you're from the Labour party.'

French schoolboy to his teacher: 'Why is the Radical Party called *radical*?'

Teacher: 'Well, because the word "radical" derives from the word "radish".'

Schoolboy: 'So?'

Teacher: 'And, as you know, a radish is red on the outside and white inside.'

Three Bulgarian crocodiles were lying on the river bank sunning themselves.

'I'm hungry,' said one. 'I could just do with a nice young child.'

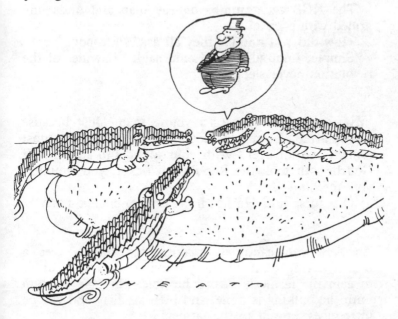

'I'm hungry too,' said the second. 'I rather fancy a nice young lady.'

The third crocodile grunted, opened one eye and said:

'I'll settle for a top Party official.'

'Why?'

'Nice and fat, and no backbone.'

In a meeting of the Supreme Soviet Council, Andropov gets a note:

'Somebody plans to kill you.'

Andropov continues his speech undisturbed. Then he receives a second note:

'The assassin is one of our leaders.'

Andropov doesn't react.

A KGB agent comes over and whispers: 'The assassin is in this room!'

Andropov lifts his eyes and says: 'Third row, second man from the left.'

The KGB agent jumps on the man and finds him armed with a pistol.

'How did you know?' they all ask Andropov.

'Simple, Comrades. As Lenin said: "Enemies of the revolution never sleep".'

'My poor mother,' cries a young man, 'Just because you've always been a Democrat doesn't mean you must remain one for ever. With your ideas, I'm sure that if God himself took the Republican ticket, you wouldn't vote for him!'

'Of course not! He has no reason to change party!'

An American candidate making the rounds sees a farmer having great difficulty milking his cow. In order to gain the farmer's favour he holds the cow for him until the milking is done, and then all dirty and wet he introduces himself to the farmer:

'I'm Mr. Jones, the Republican candidate for sheriff in the county. I suppose you know the man who's running against me.'

'Well, I reckon I do,' says the farmer. 'He must be the one in the house holding the baby.'

In a Southern bastion, that was forever Democrat, the votes are being counted. Suddenly, to the general amazement, a vote is found for the Republican candidate.

'Put it aside,' says the chief counter. 'We'll look at it later.' The counting continues, but another Republican vote appears. This time the chief smiles.

'Just as I thought! That bastard's voted twice. Annul both votes!'

What is the difference between the South African Conservative Party and the Herstigte Nasionale Party?

The Herstigte Nasionale Party wants to drive all the blacks into the sea, but the South African Conservative Party won't allow them on the beaches.

One American says to another, 'Isn't it terrible to have to choose between Carter and Ford?'

'What are you complaining about?' says another, 'We'll only get one of them.'

Party dignitaries are divided into three categories: the pedagogues, the exhibitionists, and those whose origins are obscure.

The pedagogues are those who say: 'I will teach you.'

The exhibitionists say: 'I will show you.'

Those whose origins are obscure say: 'You do not know whom you are speaking to.'

## 4 Mass media

In a country run by a fierce dictator, television viewers are delighted at last to have a chance to escape from the virtually continuous speeches of the head of state. A second television channel is announced. On the day of its opening, the dictator begins his speech on the first channel.

'Hello, yourself,' says a viewer ironically and turns the knob to switch to the other channel. On the screen there appears, rifle at the ready, a menacing policeman who says:

'Switch back to the first channel, or I'll shoot.'

An announcement on Radio Moscow: A Cadillac will be given away next week in Red Square.'

A listener telephones to check its accuracy and a correction is then announced: 'Actually it was last week, not next week; it wasn't a Cadillac but a Zim; it was Nevesky Prospekt not Red Square; and it wasn't given away, it was stolen.'

Alexander the Great, Caesar and Napoleon were rewriting history:

Alexander: 'If I had technology at my fingertips when I was alive, I would have gone to the moon and back long ago!'

Caesar: 'If I had those modern weapons, I would have conquered the entire planet.'

Napoleon: 'The Soviet news agency, Tass, would have been enough for me. Nobody would ever have known that I was defeated at Waterloo!'

The Party secretary was reporting to a meeting on his recent visit to his native village of Ivanovo, several hundred miles away in the remote steppe-land.

'I could hardly believe my eyes, comrades,' he said. 'The poverty-stricken village of my youth has now developed into a bustling industrial township. When I was a lad, before the revolution, the Ivanovo peasants lived to a man in reed-huts. Now they live in modern housing estates grouped around a magnificent Palace of Culture and a brand-new sports centre.'

Everyone was deeply impressed. When question time came round, only one old man raised his hand to speak.

'Comrade speaker, I was in Ivanovo only last week, and I didn't see any modern housing estates or Palaces of Culture. All I saw were a few reed-huts and a broken down old barn.'

'Comrade!' said the speaker severely, 'You should travel less and read *Pravda* more often.'

Question to Radio Erevan:

'Is there censorship of radio and the press in the Soviet Union?'

'In principle, no. But unfortunately it is not possible to go into this question in any detail at the present time.'

Two Russians were sitting in a factory canteen, each rolling himself a cigarette.

'What is your opinion of *Pravda*, comrade?' asked one of them.

'Admirable paper. After all, didn't Lenin himself found it?'

'And *Izvestia*?'

'Not bad. I find I get quite a lot out of it.'

'What about *Trud*?'

'To tell you the truth, I've never smoked it.'

A foreign journalist was interviewing a worker in Gdansk.

'Do you find your job rewarding?'

'In every respect.'

'And what's your apartment like?'

'Modern, spacious and cheap.'

'How do you spend your leisure?'

'I go to the opera and the theatre. I attend evening classes to broaden my education. I play football at weekends.'

'Do you possess a radio?'

'Of course I do. How else would I know how to answer your stupid questions?'

A Welsh local newspaper was very proud of being first with the news in the area. On one occasion they boasted that 'We were the first newspaper in Wales to print the news that Alderman Jones was about to resign. Later we were the first newspaper to inform its readers that this report was utterly without foundation.'

A cub reporter was sent to cover a political meeting to be addressed by the local MP but sent no copy. After the paper had gone to press he rang the news editor and said, 'I'm sorry, but the MP eloped with the wife of the constituency chairman so, as there was no speech, naturally there was no story.'

A thunder-storm was raging over London one night. Little Johnny woke up in terror and ran into his parents bedroom.

'Daddy!' he cried, shaking his father awake, 'Why is it thundering?'

'Well,' said his father, 'every time someone tells a really big lie, heaven gets angry and it thunders.'

'But isn't everyone asleep at this time of the night?'

'Yes, but it's about this time that they print the *Daily Express*.'

A *Irish Telegraph* reporter went to interview a priest in the Irish Republic but when he arrived the priest was taking confession. He waited until the end and then went into the confession box himself. 'I must confess I am from the *Irish Telegraph*,' he said.

'Brave lad,' said the priest, 'That admission must have taken real courage.'

During the 1975 Australian election campaign it became clear that Labour was flagging, so the party organizers decided that something spectacular must be done. Eventually the Party Chairman approached Gough Whitlam.

'Listen, Gough, you must do something. You've always had supreme confidence in yourself. Now if you could only walk across Lake Burley Griffin in Canberra tomorrow, it will prove what you've always thought – that you're divine – and it might just win us the election.'

So next morning, surrounded by reporters and cameramen, Whitlam stood on the shore of the lake. Everything went quiet as he put first one foot on the water . . .then the other . . . and, lo and behold, he actually walked across Lake Burley Griffin.

The Press were ecstatic. He made front page headlines. Even the most cynical newspapermen were impressed.

All except Rupert Murdoch, whose newspaper, *The Australian*, carried the following headline:
WHITLAM FAILS IN ATTEMPT TO SWIM LAKE BURLEY GRIFFIN.

---

## 5 Ideologies

An old inhabitant of Odessa aged ninety receives an inheritance of a million dollars from America. When he is told the good news, the old man does not want to hear about all this capitalist money gained through exploitation, and he refuses the inheritance. But the Soviet Union needs dollars, and so a party delegation is sent to the old man to persuade him to accept it. After several days of discussion, he finally agrees to receive his due, but he makes a condition that for one whole day all the shops of Odessa would distribute their goods free to the citizens. Despite their reservations, the party agrees, and one fine day, the shops begin the free distribution of their goods. The news spreads across the town and then the whole region. People arrive from all directions at Odessa, and by 10 o'clock all the shops are beseiged by crowds, and even the police join in. By midday, the factories in the town have closed down, since no-one is left working. By 2 o'clock there is already complete anarchy and revolution. Seeing this state of affairs, the party delegation comes to find the old man and tell what a catastrophe he has provoked.

'You see, Comrades, before I die, I wanted to know what it would be like when Communism was built in the Soviet Union.'


A West German Communist was travelling on a train through the GDR. He got into conversation with an old lady.

'Back home in West Germany,' he told her, 'shirts cost forty marks each.'

'Shirts?' said the old lady ruefully. 'We had those

here once.'

'Butter is terribly expensive in the West. We are forced to eat margarine,' he continued.

'Yes,' said the old lady, 'we had margarine here once, too.'

'Now look here!' shouted the West German, by now thoroughly exasperated, 'You don't have to tell me these fairy-stories, you know! I'm a Communist!'

'A Communist?' sighed the old lady. 'Yes, we had those here once, too.'


'What are the four stages of socialism?'
'Utopian, Scientific, Real and Curfew.'


Two Jews met in Moscow in the 1930s.

'Well, Cohen,' said one of them grimly, 'do you think we've already reached 100 per cent Communism, or will it get worse?'


'What is Socialism?'

'Socialism is the dialectical synthesis of the various stages in the historical development of mankind. From pre-history is takes the method. From antiquity, slavery. From feudalism, serfdom. From capitalism, exploitation. And from socialism, the name.'


'What is the difference between Communism and Capitalism?'

'In Capitalism man exploits man. In Communism it's vice versa'.


'Don't laugh at the bull,' remarks a royalist Spanish aristocrat. 'He knew the meaning of the red flag before any of us.'

'Have you noticed that in Mexico City the streets Insurgentes and Revolución end at Reforma?'

Shortly after the overthrow of the Fascist regime in Portugal, a wave of factory occupations swept the country. In one small Lisbon work-shop the workers told the manager, who used to be a supporter of the Salazar regime, that they would refuse him entry to the premises unless he stood for a whole day in the Rossio Square with a placard round his neck saying: 'I was a Fascist.'

The manager agreed. When he returned to the workshop, his ribs were black and blue.

'What happened?' asked one of the workers. 'Were you beaten up?'

'No,' said the manager. 'It's just that people kept on sidling up to me, digging me in the ribs and saying: "I was one too".'

'What is Zionism?'

'When one Jew persuades another to collect money from a third to send a fourth to Palestine.'

Merchant's son in Ethiopia: 'Why, father, do you look so puzzled?'

Merchant: 'Son, I have just returned from listening to Comrade Mengistu's speech to the crowd in Revolution Square. He says that soon we shall have Communism.'

Son: 'But is that so bad? When the Chairman said we would have socialism, you and I were down to our last 10 birr – and today we have more than 100,000 in the bank.'

Merchant: 'True my son, and this Communism will indeed make us millionaires. But I'm worried about the kind of wages the servants will want then.'

Two workers were arguing in the canteen in Greece.

'This is the finest country in the world,' one of them said. 'None of your puppet dictators, none of your palace revolutions. This is a democracy.'

'Democracy?' his mate replied. 'Everyone *talks* about democracy, but what do you *mean* by it?'

'I'll tell you,' said the first worker. 'You're going home late at night. You've missed your bus, it's pouring with rain and you're soaked to the skin. Just then your boss drives by. He stops the car, picks you up and takes you to his house. He lets you dry your clothes in front of his fire, gives you a big meal and a glass of his special brandy, and because it's still raining he lets you stay the night. That's democracy for you.'

'But did that ever happen to you?'

'No . . . but it happened to my sister.'


A Conservative is a fellow that if he sees someone drowning, will throw him a rope that is too short and tell him that it would be good for his character to swim for it. A Liberal will throw him a rope that's long enough, but when the drowning man gets hold of it he'll drop his end and go away to look for someone else to help.


In France under the Fourth Republic, it was a regular thing for tourists in Paris to get up early to see the changing of the government. Indeed one French deputy fell asleep in the chamber during a debate. When he woke up he asked his neighbour if anything had happened.

'Yes,' was the reply. 'You've been Prime Minister twice.'


Luigi Chiarelli was in the changing room of a famous actress, a colleague of his, where he reckoned he was sufficiently safe to express his ideas against Italian Fascism.

'How can you say that?' answers the actress, 'when the government is acting for the good of the country?'

'What?'

'And the Ministers are such honest people . . .'

'What?'

'And the Duce is far-sighted . . .'

'Listen dear, are you talking to me or are you phoning me?'

In the early years of Sadat's regime, the President was driving down a road in the presidential car, and coming to a crossroad, asked the driver:

'Which way did Nasser use to turn here?'

'Left,' replies the driver.

'OK' says President Sadat, 'signal left and turn right.'

---

## 6 Religion

A barren lady went to Chartres and told a local woman that she had undertaken the pilgrimage in the hope of being blessed with a child.

'Then you can turn back straight away,' said the woman. 'The reverend gentleman died yesterday.'

Nikolayevitch, the spaceman, lands safely back on earth. Khruschev arranges a reception. During the reception he takes Nikolayevitch to one side.

'Tell me, comrade,' he says, 'did you see God while you were up there?'

'Yes, I did.'

'Mm, I thought you would. But don't tell a soul, or you'll be in real trouble!'

A man died and went to heaven. St Peter happened to have time on his hands and offered to show the new arrival round. As they walked from place to place, St Peter pointed to the different groups and explained who they were:

'They're the Jews . . . those over there are Buddhists
. . . these are Protestants . . . the ones in the corner are
Mormons . . .'

They arrived at a compound surrounded by a high
wall. From inside could be heard the sound of voices
and laughter.

'Who are those?' asked the new arrival.

'Hush!' said St Peter, 'They're the Catholics – but
they think they're the only ones here.'

Nikolayevitch is sent on a world tour. While he is in
Rome the Pope gives him an audience.

'Tell me, Nikolayevitch,' says the Pope. 'Did you see
the Lord while you were up in Heaven?'

'No,' says Nikolayevitch.

'Mm,' says the Pope, 'I didn't think you would. But
please don't tell a soul.'

*Another, more elaborate version:*

Van der Merwe died but after two days he miraculously returned to life. At once, he was in demand all over the world. First he was summoned for an audience with the Pope.

'Did you go to heaven, my son?' the Pope asked.

'Yes,' said Van.

'And did you see God?'

'No.'

There was an intake of breath. 'Well, you mustn't ever tell anybody that. Here's a thousand dollars, and when people ask you, tell them you saw God.'

Next there was an interview with the Soviet leader Leonid Brezhnev.

'Did you go to heaven?'

'Yes.'

'And did you see God?'

'Yes,' said Van.

'For God's sake,' said Brezhnev. 'Don't ever mention that. Here's two thousand roubles, and if people ask you, tell them there is no God in heaven.'

Finally, on returning to South Africa, Van went to see the Prime Minster.

The same question came.

'Did you go to heaven, Van?'

'Yes.'

'Did you see God?'

'Yes,' said Van, holding out his hand expectantly, 'and he is Black.'

\*    \*    \*

The Queen Mother of Belgium visits Warsaw in 1956. On Sunday the functionary designated to accompany her goes with her, at her request, to Mass.

The Queen Mother asks him, 'Are you a Catholic?'

He replies with an embarrassed air: 'Believing but not practising.'

'Of course,' she exclaims, 'you are a Communist.'

'Practising,' he protests, 'but not believing.'

To gain control of the Greek Orthodox Church, the Colonels appointed a bishop who was a noted homosexual so as to use his homosexuality for blackmail as a means of controlling the Church.

A foreigner came to the monastery in Athens one day to have an audience at three o'clock in the afternoon.

He rang the bell, and the old housekeeper answered the door.

'I'd like to see Father Hieronymous,' said the foreigner.

'He's not available now. This is the time of the day when we Greeks have a siesta.'

'Oh,' said the foreigner. Then, trying to save face he adds:

'I suppose that he is in the arms of Morpheus' (the god of sleep in ancient Greece).

'I don't know the boy's name,' said the housekeeper, 'but he's a sailor of some sort!'

A bishop was arguing with a judge about who had the greater authority. 'For,' said the bishop, 'you can only condemn criminals to life imprisonment, but I can consign them to eternal damnation.'

'True,' said the judge, 'but if I send someone to prison he goes to prison.'

New England. A history lesson.

Teacher: 'Why did the Puritans leave England for America?'

A pupil: 'So that they could carry on their religion in freedom and in their way, and force others to do likewise.'

A woman phoned her bank to arrange for the disposition of a $1,000 bond. The clerk asked her:

'Madam, is the bond for redemption or conversion?'

There was a long pause: then the woman said,

'Look, am I talking to the First National Bank or the First Baptist Church?'

A marquis at the court of Louis XV unexpectedly returned from a journey and, on entering his wife's boudoir, found her in the arms of a bishop. After a moment's hesitation the marquis walked calmly to the window, leaned out and began going through the motions of blessing the people in the street.

'What are you doing?' cried the anguished wife.

'Monseigneur is performing my functions, so I am performing his.'

---

## 7 The economy

COMECON economics:

'What a beautiful dog! Is it for sale?'

'Yes, for a million lei.'

'A million lei! You're crazy, you'll never get it.'

A few days later.

'Where's the dog!'

'I sold it for one million lei.'

'Someone actually gave you a million lei for your dog?'

'Not exactly. He gave me two cats, each worth 500,000 lei.'

'What do Poland and the United States have in common?'

'In neither country can you buy anything for zlotys.'

A Hungarian economist returns from a two-year year trip to the US. The highest officials of the party interrogate him.

'What exactly did you do there?'

'Well, I studied the basis for the ineluctable death of capitalism.'

'And your conclusion?'

'Ah!' the Hungarian sighs, 'What a beautiful way to die!'

A Czech housewife says: 'Since we have a planned economy, whenever there's a shortage of ham, there's a shortage of eggs at the same time.'

A customer comes into a large food store and asks at a counter, 'Have you got any caviar?'

'Sorry,' says the assistant, 'we are the department where there is no meat. Over there is the department where they haven't got any caviar.'

A vistor comes to the door of a Russian home and asks to speak to the man of the house. A little girl answers the door and tells him that her father is not in. 'But he'll be back in eight hours, forty minutes and twenty-three seconds.'

'Where is he?' asks the visitor.

'He's orbiting the earth. He's a cosmonaut,' she tells him.

He then asks to speak to her mother. The girl explains that she is also out.

'And when will she be back?'

'Oh, I have no idea, she went to the market.'

The Minister of Agriculture is telling his friend that the Soviet Union is depressed.

'Don't worry!' says the colleague, 'All of these difficulties are temporary. There is no doubt that Communism will in the last triumph and spread throughout the world.'

The Minister (horrified): 'For heaven's sake don't say things like that. Where will we import our grain from?'

The Minister of Agriculture is on an inspection tour of collective farms. He arrives at one run by Comrade Ivanov.

'What do you feed the hens on?' asks the Minister.

'We buy in grain,' replies Ivanov.

The Minister is angry. 'How dare you when there's a grain shortage in this country? Fire him!'

The Minister arrives at a collective farm administered by a Ukranian, Galushko.

'What do you feed your hens on?' asks the Minister.

'We buy in corn,' says Galuschko.

The Minister flies into a rage. 'How dare you! We are buying corn from Canada for gold. Arrest him!'

The Minister arrives at the next farm run by a Jew, Rabinovich.

'What do you feed the hens on?' asks the Minister.

'Comrade Minister,' replies Rabinovich, 'we give them a rouble each and tell them to feed themselves.'

Question to Radio Erevan:

'What would the Soviet Union do in a totally hopeless situation?'

'We never give information over the radio about the problems of Soviet agriculture.'

Russian Jews who have lived under a planned economy all their lives find it hard to adjust to free enterprise at first. One of the new arrivals was liberally helped by the Israeli authorities to set up a barber shop. The very first morning he rang up the government office he had been dealing with.

'Your haven't sent me any customers,' he said.

Prime Minister Eshkol is addressing a meeting of workers:

'I want you to know that when I became Prime Minister the country's economy stood on the edge of an abyss. I am proud to tell you that since then we have made a brave step forward!'

Pinchas Sapir hands a coin to a beggar in New York.

'Where are you from?' asks the beggar.

'I am Israel's Finance Minister,' replies Sapir.

'Thank you very much,' says the beggar and returns the coin. 'I don't take money from colleagues.'


'Why are apples so dear?' asked the woman at the greengrocer's. 'I read in the paper that they are so plentiful that they're rotting on the trees.'

'That's just the trouble,' said the greengrocer. 'They're in short supply because it doesn't pay anyone to pick them.'

'All right, I'll have pears instead,' said the housewife.

'Sorry, no pears in the shop,' said the greengrocer. 'There's no demand.'


When prices rose sharply as a consequence of the Italy's costly war against the Abyssinians, a shopper asked his greengrocer how much the figs were:

'Three figs fifty lire,' said the greengrocer.

'Good heavens,' gasped the customer, 'how's that possible?'

'Well, sir, it isn't the figs that are worth so many lire: it's the lira that isn't worth a fig!'


A Duchess went to a Charity Ball. She ate, drank and danced all night long. She left in the early hours, and was just about to step into her Rolls when an old tramp came up to her.

'Excuse me, ma'am, could you spare a few pence – I haven't eaten for three days.'

'I've just spent all night in there to help the likes of you,' replied the Duchess. 'Aren't you people ever satisfied?'


A prominent person is about to die, and as a special

gesture he is invited to visit Heaven and Hell. He goes to Hell and sees, to his amazement, that everybody is enjoying himself with lots of food and drink. In Heaven, he finds meagre conditions, poor housing and very little to eat.

'Excuse me,' he asks his accompanying angel, 'how do you explain the subsistence conditions in Heaven?'

'We decided not to invest in a handful of people.'


Singapore in the early 1960s.

In the interests of nation-building, the Government is campaigning against expatriate employees and seeking to replace them with locals. One of the Ministers is touring the General Hospital and asks a young house-man what he is doing.

'Administering a local anaesthetic.'

'Ha!' exclaims the Minister, 'You see, we don't need those expatriates any more!'

---

## 8 The system

Brecht:

The people has failed the Government.

Therefore, we must elect a new people.


An American tourist came across a man bending over a telescope fixed on the roof of the highest building in Prague. The tourist asked the man what he was doing. The man looked cautiously around, then said:

'I'm employed by Husak personally. My job is to look through the telescope and let him know the moment I see true socialism looming up on the horizon.'

The American considered for a few seconds, then made an offer.

'Look, I can give you twice what Husak plays. All you've got to do is bring your telescope over to New York. You can stand on the Empire State building and tell me the instant you see the crisis of capitalism.'

The Czech was sorely tempted. But finally he replied:

'No, thanks all the same. I'm better off where I am. This is a job for life.'

In the 1960s the Czech Government announces its intention to establish a Ministry of the Navy. The Soviet Government responds with astonishment:

'But you have no sea coast.'

'Why is *that* a problem?' ask the Czechs. 'You have a Ministry of Justice and the Bulgarians have a Ministry of Culture.'

*Another version:*

Ben Gurion decided to appoint Sharet as Minister of the Israeli Commonwealth

'But we have no colonies,' protests Sharet.

'So what?' replies Ben Gurion, 'We have a Ministry of Finance.'

★   ★   ★

Ford was visiting Brezhnev in the Kremlin. Brezhnev was delighted to see that his guests were surprised at the opulence around them, and he couldn't resist trying to impress them still further.

He invited them into his private office. There on his desk was a golden telephone.

'Is that the hot line to Washington?' Ford asked.

'No, my friend,' replied Brezhnev. 'As a matter of fact it's my personal line to Satan.'

So saying, he picked up the phone, and within seconds he was asking the Devil to have a few words with his guests. Satan agreed, and on Ford's behalf Kissinger negotiated a similar line for the White House.

Just after they had hung up, the phone rang and Brezhnev answered it.

'Satan?' enquired Ford.

'No,' said Brezhnev, 'just the operator telling me how much the call cost.'

'And how much was it?'

'Two roubles,' Brezhnev replied, and Ford whistled in admiration.

When they returned to Washington, Ford could hardly wait to make a call to his new connection. In front of the whole Cabinet he spoke to the Devil, then put the phone down and announced that the operator would soon ring back with the cost of the call. Sure enough, a moment later the phone rang. Ford picked it up and heard the operator say:

'200 dollars.'

'200 dollars?' Ford exploded. 'But it cost Brezhnev two roubles!'

'Maybe,' said the operator, 'but that was a local call.'

An Englishman, a Frenchman and a Russian were arguing about the nationality of Adam and Eve.

'They must have been English,' declares the Englishman. 'Only a gentleman would share his last apple with a woman.'

'They were undoubtedly French,' says the Frenchman. 'Who else could seduce a woman so easily?'

'I think they were Russian,' says the Russian. 'After all, who else could walk around stark naked, feed on one apple between the two of them and think they were in paradise?'

It's 3 a.m., and Igor Abramovich is secretly studying the Bible in his apartment.

The door is suddenly kicked in, and KGB men enter. 'Why are you reading this book in Hebrew?' demanded the senior agent.

'Because when I die and go to Heaven I want to know how to speak the language.'

The agent smirked. 'And what if you go to hell?'

'I speak Russian already,' Abramovich replied.

A Polish hypnotist: 'You are in equatorial Africa, the heat is unbearable, you've had no water for days.' The volunteer sways his head and sticks his tongue out.

'You are in Siberia, it is below zero outside. You're running out of firewood.' The volunteer starts to shiver.

'You are in America. You have no work, nothing to eat, no place to sleep.' The volunteer opens one eye and says: 'You snap your finger at me and I'll break your arm.'

A young Russian woman has been on the housing list for a long time without getting a flat. In the end she succeeds in making her way to the ante-room of the boss of the local housing department, and asks to see him. The secretary has strict orders not to admit petitioners. So the young woman writes a note, puts it in an envelope and tells the secretary to take it to her boss. The note reads:

'Dear Comrade Ivan Sergeyevitch, I should like to see you personally. After all, didn't we sleep together only a fortnight ago?'

At once she is admitted to the boss, who promises to put her right at the top of the housing list. Then he looks at her in puzzlement:

'Excuse me, comrade, I'm trying to recall that occasion when we were supposed to have slept together.'

'But don't you remember – it was the week before last at our local Party meeting!'

In a political meeting in Poland the chairman asks 'Who is Gomulka?'

Silence.

'You see,' says the chairman, 'if you attended more political meetings you would know who Gomulka is.'

'Then let me ask you a question,' says a voice from the meeting. 'Do you know who Petrovich is?'

'Petrovich?' replies the Chairman, 'Can't seem to remember.'

'You see!' continues the voice, 'if you attended fewer political metings, you'd know that Petrovich is sleeping with your wife.'

Poland 1982.
A Polish boy talking to his father:
'Is it true that our Russian brothers reached the moon?'
'Yes, it is true.'
'And it is true that people can live there?'
'Not any more.'

'What is your opinion of the recent Party resolution?'
'Same as yours.'
'Then I arrest you in the name of the Secret Police.'

Comrade Kimonescu tiptoes into his flat at two o'clock one morning. As he creeps into the bedroom he sees to his horror that is wife is still awake.
'Where have you been?' she asks icily.
'What's the point of lying? There's another woman. We went out together for a meal and a drink. Then we went dancing. Then she took me back to her flat.'
'You expect me to believe that? You've been at a secret Party meeting.'

A meeting between Khruschev and Chou En Lai:
'The basic difference,' says Khruschev, between the USSR and China is that I, the son of a mere peasant, have risen to be the leader of our great country, whereas you, Comrade Chou, come from the mandarin class.'
'True,' says Chou. 'That is a basic difference. But there is also a basic similarity between us. Each of us is a traitor to his class.'

After the attempted assassination of the Pope, it is said that the KGB produced irrefutable evidence that the Pope drew his revolver first.


The Czech Party is conducting a recruitment drive.

A Party cadre is interviewing a peasant in a small country town in Moravia.

'Who were the two great founders of Scientific Socialism?'

'I don't know.'

'What do you know about Lenin?'

'Nothing, I'm afraid.'

'Who is the present leader of the great Soviet Union?'

'I haven't any idea.'

The questioning continues in similar vein. Finally the Party cadre, exasperated, asks: 'Where did you say you come from?'

'From that village over that distant hill.'

'Ahhh!' sighs the Party cadre, 'It must be a beautiful place.'


John D. Rockefeller decides to go on a vacation to Acapulco. The management of the hotel he decides to stay at are overwhelmed with excitement at the prospect, and they immediately set to work to ascertain his tastes. They discover from his aides that he likes the sand to be of a particularly fine-grained texture; that he delights in a particular shade of turquoise for the sea; and that he likes the sky to be a very special shade of azure. So they bulldoze away all the sand from the hotel beach, replacing it with sand of exactly the right texture; they inject a turquoise dye into the ocean for as far as the eye can see; and they send up helicopters to spray azure dye across the sky.

All is prepared as Rockefeller comes down to the beach from his room, a blonde on each arm. As he reclines in his deckchair, he exclaims, with unmistakable pleasure:

'You know, there are some things that money just can't buy!'


An American makes a proposal to the Vatican: he offers a hundred million dollars in exchange for the changing of one word in the Bible. He will only reveal what the word is when meeting with the Pope himself. The Curia is doubtful, but the money would certainly be useful. An audience is arranged, but it does not last long.

'What did you propose?' the puzzled cardinals ask the American.

'Only that "Amen" should be replaced by "Texas Oil".'


The moon-race had been on for over a decade. Now the moment of truth had finally arrived. After years of massive financial investment and research, the Russians and the Americans were both ready for their first manned moon-probes. As luck would have it, both landed on the moon at exactly the same time. To their utter amazement they found a Spaniard sitting inside the rim of a crater smoking a cigar.

'What's this?' asked the Russians and the Americans. 'How the hell did you get here?'

The Spaniard puffed contentedly on his cigar.

'Now look here,' fumed the Russians, 'we demand an answer!'

The Spaniard spat expertly into the crater.

'You've got no damned industry!' cursed the Americans.

'True,' answered the Spaniard. 'But we've got plenty of priests and policemen.'

'Priests and policemen? What's that got to do with it?'

'Simple. One climbs on the other's back, and so it goes on: one priest, one policeman: one priest, one policeman . . .'

A secret agent is sent to Israel. His mission is to contact Cohen in Tel Aviv. He is to identify himself by saying 'I have greetings for you from your aunt in New York' to which Cohen is to reply 'Is she well?'

The agent arrives at the address in Tel Aviv, which is an apartment block. He rings the bell marked 'Cohen' and when the door opens, gives the prearranged greeting.

'Oh, the Cohen with the aunt in New York is on the second floor,' says Cohen. So he goes to the door marked 'Cohen' on the second floor and starts his greeting again.

'Ah,' interrupts the Cohen on the second floor, 'You want Cohen the spy. Third floor.'

An English priest was on a visit to a remote part of the north of Ireland. A local farmer offered to show him the sight.

'That's Devil's Mountain,' said the farmer. 'Over there is Devil's Dyke. Devil's Wood starts on the other side of the river.'

'The Devil seems to own a lot of property in these parts,' smiled the priest.

'Aye,' agreed the farmer, 'and like most other landlords he seems to spend most of his time in London.'

An African is sitting under a coconut tree smoking his pipe when an American appears.

'Why do you just sit there doing nothing? Why don't you pull yourself together and start developing your country? You could build factories and motorways and cities. You could be a power in the world.'

'Why should I do all of that?' asks the African.

'So that you can establish yourselves as a trading nation.'

'What good would that do me?'

'Then you could make lots of money.'

'What's the good of lots of money?'
'Money will buy you leisure.'
'And what can I do with all that leisure?'
'If you have leisure, then you can rest.'
'But why do all that? I'm resting already.'

# 4 *Power and Resistance*

*What is power? How should it be defined? How is it to be identified? What does it look like? Many learned works have addressed these questions (to no great effect). But if we want to know what power feels like, above all from the recipient's point of view, there is no better evidence than political jokes. The jokes in this part – and indeed throughout the book – reveal how its victims perceive and respond to its massive presence in their lives and all the ambivalences and complexities of such perceptions and responses. They constitute rich and varied materials for a phenomenology of power as seen from below. However, freedom is what in the end these jokes are all about – as in the subtle exchange in the last joke in Section 4:*

> 'Surely you have your own opinion?'
> 'Of course I do, but I don't agree with it.'

---

## 1 The reality of revolutions

In the zoo, two monkeys, who are complaining about not having enough food to eat, decide to make a revolution. They jump on their keeper just as he brings them their meal and they strangle him to death. The director of the zoo, refusing to have them killed, decides to isolate them, and to reduce their rations for several days, to mark the event.

'There, you see,' says the female to the male monkey, looking sadly at the half-dozen bananas destined to serve as their meal for the day. 'I still think it was better under the old regime.'

During the French Revolution, the Secretary of State of the King's Household, Chrétien de Lamoignon de Malesherbes, was condemned to be guillotined.

While mounting the scaffold, he stumbles and falls.

'An ancient Roman would have seen that as a bad omen,' he remarks, 'and would have returned home.'


A census is being taken in Leningrad and an elderly citizen is answering questions:

'Where were you born?'

'St Petersburg.'

'Where were you educated?'

'Petrograd.'

'Where do you live?'

'Leningrad.'

'Where will you die?'

'St Petersburg.'


'After the Revolution, everyone will have strawberries and cream.'

'But I don't like strawberries and cream.'

'After the Revolution, you will like strawberries and cream.'


An old woman asks her granddaughter: 'Grand-daughter, please explain Communism to me. How will people live under it? They probably teach you about it in school.'

'Of course they do, Grandma. When Communism comes, the shops will be full – there'll be butter, and meat and sausage . . . you'll be able to go out and buy anything you want . . .'

'Ah!' exclaims the old woman joyously. 'Just like under the Tsar!'


A Polish peasant visited Warsaw for the first time since

before the war. He was looking for an old friend whose address he carried on a faded slip of paper. But the city had changed a great deal since his last visit, and he was hopelessly lost. So he stopped to ask a policeman:

'Excuse me, comrade, can you tell me how to get to Pilsudski Square?'

'Pilsudski Square? It's not called that any more. It's called Stalin Square now.'

'Oh. Well, could you tell me the way to Sapieha Street, then?'

'It's not called that any more. It's called Molotov Street now.'

'Oh, I see,' said the peasant, who was by now totally confused.

He walked on through the town, until at last he came to the river. Standing on the embankment, he gazed mournfully into the water. Meanwhile, his suspicions aroused, the policeman had followed the peasant.

'Hey! What do you think you're doing now?' he demanded.

'I'm just taking a look at the Volga.'

A streetcar in Moscow after the Revolution.

'Lenin Square,' announces the conductor.

'Formerly Nicholas Square,' mutters a Jewish passenger.

The conductor gives him a warning look and announces, 'Street of the October Revolution.'

'Formerly Street of Peter the Great,' says the Jew.

Now the conductor gets very annoyed and shouts 'Watch your tongue, Comrade Israelite.'

'Formerly dirty Jew,' comments the passenger.

Lenin has died and appears at St Peter's gate. He is admitted on trial, and St Peter is told to keep an eye on him. After a week or so, God asks him, 'Well, Peter, how's Lenin's re-education progressing?'

'Fine, Comrade God,' answers St Peter.

Stalin and Nicholas the Second meet in hell. The Tsar asks Stalin what changes were introduced after the revolution.

'Have you still got an army?'

'We've got a bigger and better army than ever before. We have six million men under arms.'

'And have you still got a secret police?'

'Of course. Our MVD would put your Ochrana to shame, I can assure you!'

'And do you still have enough Cossacks to maintain law and order?'

'Regiments of them!'

'What about vodka?'

'Gallons of the stuff!'

'Is it still 40 per cent proof?'

'It's 42 per cent now!'

'And do you think the whole thing was worth it – just for that 2 per cent?'


Brezhnev's mother came to visit her son.

'This is my house,' said Brezhnev, showing her around. 'And this is my car. And that's my swimming pool. And this' – he shows her some photographs – 'is my second house. And this is my aeroplane. And this is my villa on the Black Sea. And this is my yacht.'

His mother gasps in wonder.

'You do well, son,' she says. 'But I'm worried for you. What if the Bolsheviks come back?'


Khruschev is ninety years old. He lives in a dacha near Moscow but is not permitted to leave it. Meanwhile, Russia has undergone profound changes. In the Kremlin, there lives once more the Tsar of all the Russias. But Khruschev feels death approaching. He wants to see his capital one last time. So he telephones the Tsar.

'It's Nikita here,' he says. 'I'm old. Grant me permission to come to Moscow. I wish to see our beautiful capital before I die. I promise to behave and speak to no one.'

The Tsar turns and asks: 'Well, what do you think, Mikoyan?'


Stalin one day questions his driver.

'Are you more or less happy than before the Revolution?'

'Less happy,' says the driver.

'And why?'

'Before the Revolution, I had two suits, while today I only have one.'

'What are you complaining about?' says Stalin. 'In Africa people live completely naked.'

'Ah!' says the driver, 'and when did they have their revolution?'


A school class in a Communist country.

The teacher says to the class:

'There are many different roads to Communism: the Russian, the Chinese, the Yugoslav, the Polish.'

One of the students responds: 'Why do all roads lead to Communism, but no road leads from Communism.'


A lady asks a South American diplomat: 'What is your favourite sport in Latin America?'

'Bullfighting.'

'Revolting!'

'No, ma'am,' says the diplomat, 'revolting is our second sport.'


Castro is visiting Nicaragua. The Sandinista leadership takes him to the beach. After his tour they ask him what he would like for dinner.

'Just my usual rice and beans will be fine,' he says. They laugh and insist he try the fried shrimp and

broiled lobster. The next day in León the same thing:
'Just some tortillas and salt will be more than enough,' says the Cuban leader.

Again, his hosts laugh and order thick flank cuts of beef. His last night in Managua, he asks for only Cuban-style rice and a glass of water, but instead they serve him a delicious twelve-course meal.

Finally Castro flies home to Havana, where the central committee of the party is waiting for him at the airport.

'So tell us, how goes the Nicaraguan revolution?' they ask.

'Well, Comrades,' replies Castro, 'to be honest, the Nicaraguan revolution seems to be where we were twenty years ago.'

Soviet scientists had developed a technique for bringing embalmed corpses back to life and were immediately set to work on Lenin. So that he could catch up with what had happened since his death, it was decided to confine him to a room stocked with all the back numbers of *Pravda*. Meals were passed in to him through a hatch in the wall. After this had gone on for several weeks, it was noticed that the last few meals had not been eaten, and knocks on the door yielded no reply. When the room was unlocked Lenin was nowhere to be found. The window was wide open and on the desk lay a note bearing the words:
GONE TO SWITZERLAND. WE MUST BEGIN AGAIN.

## 2 Arbitrary power

A Nazi concentration camp.

A guard promises a prisoner his freedom if he can identify which of the guard's eyes is the glass one. The prisoner answers without hesitation, 'It is your left one.'

'How do you know?'

'It is the only one that shows any trace of human sympathy.'


An American and a Russian argue about freedom in their countries.

'We in America enjoy real freedom,' the American says, 'I can stand in front of the White House and shout that President Reagan is a fool and nothing will happen to me.'

'So what?' replies the Russian, 'I can stand on Red Square and shout that President Reagan is a fool and nothing will happen to me, either.'


In a fishing session in the company of Hitler and Mussolini, Chamberlain, the British Prime Minister, patiently pays out his line, lights his pipe and within two hours has hauled in a large catch, after which the Duce hurls himself headlong into the pond and grabs a fat pike. When it is Hitler's turn, he orders all the water to be drained out of the pond. Seeing the fish thrash about helplessly on the dry bed, Chamberlain asks 'Why don't you scoop them up?'

Hiltler replies, 'They have to beg me first.'


Three Soviet labour camp inmates sit chatting.

'What are you in for?' asks the first.

'Me? I spoke badly of Comrade Popov in 1939.'

'And you?'

'I spoke well of Comrade Popov in 1940.'

'And what about you?,' they asked turning to the third.

'I am Comrade Popov.'


A Russian meets an old friend on a Moscow Street after many years.

'But where have you been?' he asks.

'In prison,' the other replies.

'How terrible! For how long?'

'Ten years.'

'But what for?'

'Nothing, of course,' his friend replies.

'No,' he says, 'that is impossible. You only get *five* years for nothing.'


A Jew in Moscow was awakened in the middle of the night by a loud knock on the door.

'Who's there?' he called.

'The postman!' came the reply.

The man got out of the bed and opened the door and found two KGB agents.

'Are you Goldstein?'

'Yes.'

'And did you make an application to go to Israel?'

'That's right.'

'Do you have enough food to eat here?'

'Yes, we do.'

'Don't your children get a good Communist education?'

'Certainly.'

'Then why do you want to leave Russia?'

'Because,' replied Goldstein, 'I don't like the post being delivered at three in the morning.'


A commission visited a school to investigate the inculcation of patriotism among its pupils.

'Boris,' asked a member of the commission, 'who is your father?'

'My father is the Soviet Union,' replied Boris.

'Good boy! And who is your mother?'

'The Communist Party,' replied Boris.

'Good boy! And what do you want to be when you grow up?'

'An orphan.'

An old Jew made an illegal attempt to flee the Soviet Union. He was caught at the border and interrogated by the KGB.

'Citizen Rabinovitch, what made you decide to try and escape?' asked the interrogator.

'I have two reasons,' replied Rabinovich. 'Firstly, if the Soviet government collapses, everyone will blame us, the Jews.'

'Don't talk such foolishness!' shouted the interrogator. 'The Soviet government is stronger than ever! It will never collapse!'

'That's my other reason.'


Among the trouble-makers under Stalin's rule was Krupskaya, the widow of Lenin, but even Stalin could not afford to have her 'liquidated'. He summoned her, and threatened:

'If you don't stop criticizing me, I'll have someone else appointed Lenin's widow!'


A group of tourists visits the Kremlin. As they feast their eyes on the display of the world's most fabulous and valuable jewels, one of the guests asks in astonishment:

'Shouldn't you keep such priceless treasures under lock and key?'

'In the Soviet Union,' replies the guide, 'the most priceless treasure is man.'


A Russian and a Chinese are discussing the idea of peaceful co-existence. According to the Russian, it is entirely possible for capitalism and socialism to live peacefully side by side. The Chinese vehemently disputes this.

In order to prove his point, the Russian takes him to Moscow zoo, where a lamb and a wolf are kept together in the same cage.

'Just as the lamb and the wolf lie down together,' says the Russian, 'so two opposed social systems can live peacefully on the same planet.'

The Chinese is deeply impressed.

'But how on earth do you manage it?' he asks. 'A wolf and a lamb in the same cage!'

'It's simply a question of organization,' answers the Russian. 'We put a new lamb in each morning.'


A Pole has returned from the USSR.

'How were things over there?' he's asked.

'Not too bad,' he says. 'I couldn't complain.'

'Well then why are you back?'

'What a question. Here at least I can complain!'


When the censors closed down the Warsaw theatre production of *Dziady* (the famous drama by Poland's greatest nineteenth-century poet Mickiewicz), thereby igniting the student riots of March 1968, Gomulka called in General Moczar.

'Couldn't you, comrade, have had a little talk with that fellow Mickiewicz and had him change some of the passages in his comedy so that it followed our Party line a bit more? We would have avoided all this trouble.'

'But my dear comrade,' cries Moczar, 'Mickiewicz is dead!'

'That's very bad, comrade. Why are you always in such a hurry?'


Three bears, one American, one Russian and one Czech discuss their respective lives. The American bear, who comes from Alaska, bemoans his lot:

'A bear can't lead a decent life anymore, what with the highways and petrol fumes and noise and advertising everywhere.'

The Russian bear is no less unhappy:

'Siberia is no place any more for a self-respecting bear,

what with the Komsomal brigades everywhere and the drab apartment blocks and queues for meat.'

But the Czech bear is much more cheerful:

'Life is not so bad, really. I come from the High Tatras but in 1969 I was expelled from the Czechoslovak Federation of Bears and sent to the treeless plains of Southern Bohemia where I have been employed ever since as a cuckoo.'


'Are there any historical precedents for the Soviet system of elections?'

'Yes, in the story of the Creation, God made Eve, put her in the Garden of Eden, and said to Adam: 'Now choose a woman'.'


The Iranian secret police, Savak, carries out a search of a student hostel looking for subversive literature. They enter the room of one student and find nothing incriminating. The much-relieved student is horrified when an agent opens a final cupboard in which there hangs a picture of Marx. The agent turns to the student and admonishes him.

'I can't understand you kids today. I know you don't care about jeopardizing yourself, but at least you could spare a thought for your poor old father.'


In South Korea a civil rights activist protests to the head of the security branch about the lack of democracy.

'Quite right,' says the Security Chief, 'President Chin believes firmly in civilian rule. So, as soon as a military man obtains political office, he must take off his uniform.'


A demonstration of Communists was held in the United States and the police were called to disperse the demonstrators. They started to beat everyone and one

demonstrator called to the policeman,
'Don't beat me. I am an anti-communist.'
'I don't care what kind of Communist you are!' says
the policeman.


A Czech and a Dutchman are talking about housing
problems in their respective countries.
Dutchman: 'Housing problems we Dutch can understand, but what must be so terrible for you is not having
freedom of speech to complain about them.'
Czech: 'But we do have freedom of speech!'
Dutchman: 'What do you mean?'
Czech: 'We are free to say absolutely anything we
like. The only difference is that we don't have freedom
*after* speech!'


The Emperor Ghengis Khan, hearing of the legendary
Nasrudin, decides to visit him in person. Nasrudin
offers him, as a gift, a basket of figs. The Emperor
starts to fling them, one by one, at Nasrudin's head.
Nasrudin merely smiles, and the Emperor demands to
know why.
'Because I was thinking of offering you water
melons.'


---

## 3 Repression

In a small village in the Ukraine, a terrifying rumour
was spreading: a Christian girl had been found
murdered. Realizing the dire consequences of such an
event, and fearing a pogrom, the Jewish community
instantly gathered in the synagogue to discuss whatever
defensive actions were possible under the circumstances.
Just as the emergency meeting was being called to
order, in ran a man, out of breath and all excited.

'Brothers,' he cried out, 'I have wonderful news! The murdered girl is Jewish!'

At the 20th Party Congress as Khruschev recounted the evils perpetrated by Stalin, a voice called from the hall:
    'And where were you then?'
    'Would the man who asked that question please stand up,' said Khruschev.
    Silence. Nobody stands up.
    'That's where we were too!' replied Khruschev.

It is 1937. There are mass arrests in the Soviet Union. People live in fear, every night expecting to be carted away . . .
    One night there is a loud knocking at the door of a certain house. The tenants cower in silence afraid to answer it. The knocking continues, getting louder and louder. The tenants go on pretending to be asleep. Finally someone begins to break the door down. At this, one tenant thinks to himself,
    'I'm an old man. I've got to die soon anyway. What am I afraid of? I'll open up to them.'
    He gets out of bed and goes to the door. A minute later he rushes back shouting for joy.
    'Comrades, get up! It's only a fire . . .'

A man in Johannesburg was bothered by a tom-cat which kept the neighbourhood awake at night with its loud pursuit of female cats. The man was advised by a friend to have the animal neutered. He did so. Some time later, his friend came around to ask if this had done the trick.
    'Well,' the man replied, 'he is still making a lot of noise, but now merely in an advisory capacity.'

A French peasant taught her parrot to say 'Mort aux Boches.' A Gestapo agent heard the bird and warned the peasant that she would be sent to a concentration camp if the parrot ever repeated the phrase. The peasant sought the advice of the village curé and the curé suggested a swap with his own perfectly bred parrot. When the Gestapo man came he waited and waited but the parrot said nothing. Finally the agent, himself, shouted 'Mort aux Boches!' and the parrot answered very softly, 'May the Lord answer your prayers, my son.'

Brezhnev is dining in a restaurant. The waiter brings the first course.
'Haven't I seen you somewhere before?'
'No.'
'Wasn't it in Odessa in 1938?'
'No.'
The waiter brings the second course.
'Are you sure I haven't seen you before? Was it perhaps in the Ukraine in 1952?'
'No.'
The waiter brings the last course.
'I'm sure I have seen you before,' Brezhnev insists. 'Didn't you bring me the first course?'

'There are,' an American politican proclaimed loudly, 'two things I detest above all else – prejudices and niggers.'

During the American Civil War an old negro took a great interest in the conflict but showed no signs of wanting to take part in it. A white man asked him one day.
'The men of the northern and southern states are killing one another on your account. Why don't you join in and fight yourself?'
'Have you ever seen two dogs fighting over a bone?'

the negro demanded.
'Yea, many times,' the white man answered.
'Did you ever see the bone fight?'


A lieutenant, two white soldiers and a black soldier are
flying in an American air-force jet when something goes
wrong with the plane. There are only four parachutes.
The lieutenant announces that since he is in charge,
he will take one of the parachutes, and in order to
determine which of the three soldiers will take the
remaining two parachutes, he will ask the soldiers
questions and the first to answer incorrectly will remain
on the crashing plane. He asks the first white soldier:
'In what year and on what country did the United
States drop the atom bomb in World War Two?' The
white soldier answers:
'1945, on Japan.'
Then he asks the second white soldier:
'Which cities were bombed and how many people
were killed?'
The second white soldier also answers correctly.
Then, the lieutenant asks the black soldier:
'Give me all the names and addresses of those killed.'


Two Jews are walking in Nazi Germany through an
anti-semitic neighbourhood one evening, when they
notice they are being followed by a pair of hoodlums.
'Sam,' says his friend, 'we better get out of here.
There are two of them and we're alone!'


Israel wins the war against the Soviet Union. At the
head of his victorious army, Begin liberates Moscow.
He asks the rejoicing crowds what is their most urgent
wish. They answer with one voice: 'Give Goldberg back
his party card.'

The body of a Catholic was found on the Falls Road in Belfast with seventeen bullet-holes in him.

The Protestant coroner said at the inquest that it was the worst case of suicide he'd ever come across.

Stalin has just explained his plans:

'Those who agree please raise your right hands. And as for those who do not agree, please turn your faces to the wall, with your hands in the air, and wait.'

A South American dictator delegates an ambassador to the dictator of a neighbouring state to discover the secret of his success. Without saying a word, the dictator leads the diplomat to a cornfield.

Thereafter, every time he sees a sheaf of corn rising above the others, he cuts its head off.

'Why is the profession of dentistry the most desperate in China?'

'To have 800 million potential clients – all afraid to open their mouths!'

*Another version:*

A British soldier and a Russian soldier went fishing in the same river which marked the border between zones East and West. The British soldier was hauling out fish by the dozen, the Russian soldier caught nothing. Eventually Alexei could stand it no longer.

'Vot is ze secret of your success and my failure?' he asked.

'Quite simple,' said Tommy. 'It's only on this side of the river that the fish dare open their mouths.'

\*   \*   \*

A Soviet composer was sitting in a train, engrossed in a score of music. A policeman got into his carriage, noticed him reading, and immediately became suspicious.

'What's that you're reading there?' he asked menacingly.

'Oh this?' replied the composer with a nervous smile. 'It's a Tchaikovsky overture.'

'What do you take me for? It's a secret code, and you are a spy! Come with me to headquarters.'

When they arrived at headquarters, the composer once again insisted that what he was reading was the score of a Tchaikovsky overture. At this point the chief interrogator leaned menacingly over his desk and shouted:

'We've had enough of your lies! You might just as well tell us everything – your friend Tchaikovsky has already confessed.'

*Another version:*

It was rumoured in Budapest that the secret police had dredged up a mysterious three-fold coffin from the bed of the Danube. Legend has it that Attila the Hun was buried there in such a coffin.

'The man in the coffin is definitely Attila the Hun,' people told each other.

'But how can you be so sure?'

'He confessed.'

★ ★ ★

'How did the poet Mayakovsky die?'
'Suicide.'
'What were his last words?'
'Don't shoot, comrades!'

In the later stages of the war when the occupying Germans robbed and starved Holland to feed themselves, a Dutchman passes a railway siding where a herd of cows is being driven into cattle trucks. He asks a railwayman what is going on.

'Some unknown cow bit through a military telephone wire and now fifty cows are being taken to Germany as hostages.'

A Zionist tries to convince an old Russian Jew to emigrate to Israel.

'This is not for me,' says the Jew. 'I am eighty-six years old and how many years will God give me in Israel, two or three?'

'But why stay here?'

'In Russia,' says the Jew, 'I can just say a few words and get at least fifteen years.'

1930. The world is in the throes of an international crisis of capitalism. Fritz is thinking of leaving the grinding poverty of Germany and emigrating to the Soviet Union, the working people's paradise. His friend Hans is also attracted to the idea, but he is cautious and still has reservations.

'All right, then,' says Fritz, 'I'll go first and write back and tell you what it's like. Then you can come over and join me.'

'But perhaps they have censorship,' says Hans. 'I'll tell you what – if everything is all right, use normal coloured ink. But if you want to convey to me that what you're writing is not true, then use green ink.'

Fritz makes his way to the Soviet Union. Three months later Hans gets a letter from him:

'Everything is just fine. There's plenty to eat and plenty to drink. I've been given a big, airy apartment and a couple of suits of clothing. I'm thinking of buying a motor-bike soon. This summer I'm off to the Black Sea for my holidays. Don't believe anything you read in the capitalist press about the Soviet Union – it's all lies. You can get everything you need here. The only thing you can't get is green ink.

Yours sincerely, Fritz.'

The Master of a Belfast Orange Lodge was driving home from a parade one evening when he saw two men walking down a lane wearing shamrocks in their button-holes. Incensed at the sight, he drove straight into them. One went hurtling through his windscreen, the other flew head over heels into a ditch.

An officer of the Royal Ulster Constabulary came hurrying up to the scene of the 'accident'.

'Are you all right, sir?' he asked, seeing the driver's orange sash.

'Sure I'm all right, but what about these two Fenians?'

'Don't you worry, sir. We'll charge this one with breaking and entering, and that one with running away from the scene of the crime.'


Two officers are strolling down the street five minutes before the military curfew in Poland when a man walks by. One officer turns and shoots him on the spot.

'Why did you do that?' his colleague asks. 'He still has five minutes to go!'

'Yeah,' says the first, 'But I know him – he lives fifteen minutes away.'


Andropov is sitting at Brezhnev's bedside just as the dying leader is about to breathe his last breath. But Brezhnev opens his eyes and says:

'I must warn you Yuri, it won't be easy to get the Soviet people to follow you once I am gone.'

Andropov smiles and says: 'Don't worry Leonid. Those who don't follow me will follow you.'


Carlos Vides Casnova, El Salvador's Minister of Defence, is out fishing with his Joint Chiefs of Staff, but they have had no luck, not a bite all day. Finally Vides Casanova pulls up a fish, but it's very small, only about six inches long.

'That's it,' he announces, unhooking the fish, 'I'll throw this one back and we call it a day.'

'Please, my general, give me the fish,' says the colonel sitting next to him.

'But it's a very small fish,' the Defence Minister replies.

'Please, my general.'

'Well, all right,' and Vides Casanova hands over the fish.

The colonel takes its head in one hand and begins slapping it with the open palm of his other hand.

'Where are the big ones?' he shouts. 'Tell us where the big ones are!'

Poland (in the first days of military rule).

In the early hours of the morning, there is a knock at the door.

'Who is there?'

'The milkman.'

'You lie.'

'No, the militia never lies.'

## 4 The ambiguities of quiescence

Two Jews are about to enter the gas chamber in Auschwitz. One of them turns to the SS guard to make a last request for a glass of water.

'Hymie,' says his friend, 'don't make trouble.'

Kohn and Goldstein meet in Berlin. Kohn tells Goldstein that Davidsohn has died. Goldstein shrugs his shoulders:

'Well, if he got a chance to better himself . . .'

In Treblinka, where the prisoners were employed to carry gassed corpses of inmates to the crematorium, prisoners who ate too much would be told: 'Hey, Moise, don't overeat! Think of us who have to carry you!'

'Why did the Germans represent a medical miracle in the Nazi era?'
'Because they were able to walk round upright with a broken backbone'.

Altmann and his secretary were sitting in a coffeehouse in Berlin in 1935.
'Herr Altmann,' said his secretary, 'I notice you're reading *Der Stürmer*. I can't understand why you're carrying a Nazi libel sheet. Are you some kind of masochist, or, God forbid! a self-hating Jew?'
'On the contrary, Frau Epstein. When I used to read the Jewish papers, all I learned about were pogroms, riots in Palestine, and assimilation in America. But now that I read *Der Stürmer* I see so much more: that the Jews control all the banks, that we dominate in the arts, and that we're on the verge of taking over the entire world. You know, it makes me feel a whole lot better!'

A Jew walks along the street of Berlin and mutters:
'Damn the Führer . . .'
A stormtrooper stops him:
'How dare you . . .'
The man replies:
'I don't mean *your* Führer. I mean *ours*. If the damned fool hadn't let us out of Egypt we would all have a chance of becoming British subjects.'

An Irishman got mixed up in a riot and was surrounded by a group of heavily armed men who asked what his religion was. He didn't know whether his questioners were Catholics or Protestants but he could see that they all carried weapons, so he said:
'Sure, I'm of the same opinion as the big fellow over there with that axe.'

A visitor to Northern Ireland breaks his spectacles and goes to an optician, who tells him they can't be repaired for six weeks.

'But can't you do it any sooner?' he asks.

'Well,' he replies, 'we could always board them up for you.'

'What is the difference between the Prague Uprising and the film of the Prague Uprising?'

'The film was five minutes shorter.'

A man knocked at the door of a shabby Moscow apartment. On the door was a plate with the name 'Rabinovich' on it. After a while a dishevelled-looking man of indeterminate age answered the door.

'Yes?'

'Does the tailor Rabinovich live here?'

'No.'

'Who are you, then?'

'Rabinovich.'

'Then why did you say you didn't live here?'

'You call this living?'

First it was Tsarism, with all its indescribable misery. Then it was Stalinism, with all the crimes that went with it. And today? What is it today?

Monday.

The Bishop Graf Galan is giving a sermon in the Cathedral in which he is preaching against the education of young people in the Hitler Jugend. Someone shouts from the crowded congregation: 'How can a man who has no children dare to preach about the education of children?'

To which Galan replies: 'I cannot allow such personal criticism of the Führer in my church.'

Elated by his victory over Antony at Actium, Augustus Caesar comes back to Rome. One of those flocking to congratulate him has a crow which he has taught to say: 'Hail, Caesar victorious!' Augustus is impressed and buys the bird for a large sum of money. But a partner of the bird's trainer, who has received nothing, tells Augustus that the man has another crow and urges the Emperor to make him produce it. When the bird is produced, it declares: 'Hail, Antony victorious!'

A Jewish member of a Soviet delegation abroad makes a number of speeches entirely following the official party line on all matters. At one meeting a Jewish member of the audience asks him his opinions about Israel, and he gives the orthodox answers about Zionist imperialism, etc.

Afterwards the questioner takes him aside and says,

'Surely you, you're a Jew, surely you have your own opinion about these matters?'

'Of course I do,' says the Soviet Jew, 'but I don't agree with it.'

---

## 5 Resistance

Every Sunday Brigadier General Afrain Rios Montt presided at a big revival service on the edge of Guatemala City. Sometimes he had born-again US astronauts preach to his congregation; other times, reformed guerrillas or Catholics. One day he pulled in the biggest crowd of all when Jesus Christ himself agreed to appear.

Christ walks on stage and tells the assembled throng,

'I'd just like to thank the general for inviting me here today. Personally I feel very close to the general.'

This gets a big cheer.

'If you look in our eyes you will see the same visionary light.'

More cheering.

'We are about the same size, height and weight.'

Still more cheering and shouts of Hallelujah.

'In fact Rios Montt and I are practically one and the same person.'

A huge roar: 'So why don't you crucify the son of a bitch?'


The Basque Country.

A man goes to confession:

'Father, I have sinned. I have killed the Spanish Chief of Police.'

'Son, make your confession first, then you can turn to boasting.'


God, disappointed with mankind's performance since Noah, decides upon a second Flood, to take place in thirty days' time. He commands the Archangel Gabriel to inform the leaders of the world religions of the impending end of the world.

First Gabriel visits Mecca and tells the bad news to the elders gathered round the Kaaba. They immediately determine to pray to Allah for the next thirty days. Gabriel next visits Rome and, granted an audience with the Pope, gives him the bad news. The Pontiff orders all Catholics to repent their sins, but, in the circumstances, urges them to make the best of their remaining days on earth.

Finally, the Archangel visits the Jewish ghetto in Rome and conveys his message to the rabbi, who asks:

'Is it really so?'

'Alas, yes.'

'Is it to be fire or water?'

'Water.'

'Will it be twenty metres, fifty metres or seventy metres deep?'

'Seventy, I'm afraid.'

'Oh well,' sighs the rabbi, 'We'll just have to learn to live under water!'

Moses was recruited to the Prussian army.

The officer comes for inspection and when he sees Moses he asks him:

'Tell me, why should a soldier sacrifice his life for the Fatherland?'

Moses: 'You are quite right, officer, why should he?'

Czechoslovakia:

A man shouting in Prague: 'The Russians have landed on the moon!'

Passerby: 'Really? All of them?'

Trying to improve business a little, a Munich street-trader held up his wares and cried:

'Buy your fish here. Every one as fat as Goering.'

But a member of the SS heard him. He was arrested and jailed for twelve months. On being released, he went back to his old trade.

'Buy your fish here. Every one as fat as . . .' He stopped short, seeing his old friend from the SS.

'Go on. As fat as what?' the Nazi asked menacingly.

'As fat as last year,' the trader replied.

An elderly Jew in Berlin finds himself surrounded by a group of Nazis, who knock him to the ground and demand:

'So, who is responsible for the War?'

The Jew immediately replies:

'The Jews and the bicycle riders.'

'Why the bicycle riders?'

'Why the Jews?'

A Jew, crossing the street, bumped into a Nazi.

'Swine!' bellowed the Nazi.

'Goldberg,' bowed the Jew.

Two Jews had a plan to assassinate Hitler. They learnt that he drove by a certain corner at noon each day, and they waited for him there with their guns well hidden. At exactly noon they were ready to shoot, but there was no sign of Hitler. Five minutes later, nothing. Another five minutes went by, but no sign of Hitler. By 12.15 they started to give up hope.

'My goodness,' said one of the men. 'I hope nothing's happened to him!'

Freudenheim was walking down the street in Nazi Germany in 1934, when suddenly a large black limousine pulled up beside him. Freudenheim looked up in astonishment and terror as Hitler himself climbed out of the car. Holding a gun to Freudenheim, Hitler ordered him to get down on his hands and knees and pointing to a pile of excrement on the kerb, ordered the Jew to eat it.

Freudenheim, putting discretion before valour, complied.

Hitler began laughing so hard that he dropped the gun. Freudenhiem picked it up and ordered Hitler to undergo the same humiliation. As Hitler got down on the sidewalk, Freudenheim ran away from the scene as fast as he could.

When Freudenheim got home, his wife asked him:

'How was your day?'

'Oh, fine,' he answered, 'the usual sort of day . . . but you'll never guess who I had lunch with!'

A new maid is being engaged by a well-to-do Roman lady. The wage she is offered is not very generous:

'All right,' she says, 'but I want a bonus for keeping my mouth shut when you have insulted the Duce.'

'That won't help you much,' replies the lady. 'In this house the Duce is never insulted.'

'Well then, I want a bonus for keeping quiet about your supplies from the black market.'

'You're wrong again, we never buy on the black market.'

'Then I want a bribe for not informing the *Ovra* (secret police) that you're listening to the Italian programme of the BBC.'

'We'd never listen to it.'

'So what kind of a job is this?'

A Russian and a Jew are sentenced to death. The prison warden calls them in to grant each a final wish.

'What is yours?' he asks the Russian.

'I want to make a confession.'

'Very well,' says the warden, 'A priest will be brought.'

He turns to the Jew. 'And what is yours?'

'Before I die, I want to eat a bowl of strawberries and cream.'

The warden is astonished. 'Where will we find strawberries and cream in Siberia in the winter?'

'There's no hurry, Comrade Warden. I can wait.'

Italy under Mussolini.

A woman goes to the market. There are long queues for pasta and fruit. There is no bread, no cheese and no soap.

'It's all his fault,' she shouts for all to hear. 'That swine! That jumped-up little pickpocket!'

A man from the secret police marches up to her.

'One moment, signora. Who are you referring to?'

The woman takes a step back, clearly terrified. But she manages to regain her presence of mind.

'Why . . .' she stutters, 'my husband, of course!'

The secret policeman's face drops. He turns as white as a sheet, and salutes the woman respectfully.

'Please accept my humble apologies. I really didn't recognise you, Donna Rachele.'

*Another version:*

In Stalin's Moscow a man is running along the street shouting:

'The whole world is suffering because of one man! One man!'

He is seized and dispatched to the KGB. There he is taken to the interrogation room.

'What were you shouting in the streets?' asks the interrogator.

'I was shouting that the whole world suffers because of one man.'

'And who did you have in mind?' The interrogator's eyes narrow.

'What do you mean, who?' The man is astonished. 'Hitler, naturally.'

'Ahh . . .' smiles the interrogator. 'In that case you are free to leave.'

The man walks the length of the room, reaches the door, opens it and suddenly stops and turns around to face the interrogator.

'Excuse me, but who did *you* have in mind?'

\*      \*      \*

Once there was a Greek general who had a parrot which he taught to drink brandy, and he also taught the parrot to say 'Long live Papadopoulos!'

After the Junta fell in 1974, the general told the parrot: 'Don't say "Long live Papadopoulos" any more or I'll have to put you in jail!'

One night the general gave a party at his house, and during the evening some of the guests started giving brandy to the poor parrot and got him drunk! Suddenly, the drunken parrot started shrieking:

'Long live Papadopoulos! Long live Papadopoulos!'

So the general put the parrot in prison.

Inside the prison there were a lot of men. One of the men said,

'I'm in here for killing a man.'

Another man said, 'I'm in here for stealing.'

Then the men turned to the parrot and asked,

'What are *you* in here for?'

'I'm in here,' said the parrot, 'because of my political opinions!'


When Papadopoulos came to power, he decided that there should be new Greek postage stamps issued with his portrait. The new stamps were printed and put into circulation, but there were many complaints about the stamps because they did not adhere to the envelopes. Papadopoulos called the head of the Greek Post Office to his office and said:

'Look, there's nothing wrong with these stamps. I lick them and they stick.'

The man said, 'Maybe the trouble is that the people have been spitting on the wrong side of the stamps!'


A Russian Jew fell off the river bank into the water. Since he could not swim, he was in danger of drowning.

Two Tsarist policemen heard cries for help and rushed to the river bank. But when they saw that it was a Jew, they laughed at him and began to walk off.

'Help, I can't swim,' shouted the Jew.

'Well, drown then.'

Suddenly the Jew shouts with his last breath:

'Down with the Tsar.'

The policemen immediately sprang into the river, pulled him on to the bank and arrested him for sedition.


Generalissimo Francisco Franco falls in the river and is on the point of drowning. At the last moment a man jumps in and rescues him. Only after he has pulled the half-drowned dictator to the river bank is he aware of his identity. In order to show his gratitude, Franco grants the man a wish.

'I have only one wish,' says his rescuer. 'Don't tell a soul that it was me that pulled you out.'

Hitler – who was superstitious and had his own astrologer – arranging a spiritualist seance to call the spirit of Moses into his presence. Moses appears.

'How did you manage to divide the waters of the Red Sea?' asks Hitler. 'I should like to use the same method for crossing the English Channel.'

'Well,' replies Moses, 'all I had to do was to touch the waters with my magic rod.'

'And where can I find that rod now?' asks Hitler.

'In the British Museum.'

It comes to the notice of the Führer that there is rabbi in Theresienstadt concentration camp gifted with prophetic powers. He has the man brought before him.

'Who will win the war?'

'I must first consult the oracle,' answers the rabbi.

'Oracle? Which oracle?'

'I toss a coin, Herr Hitler. If it comes out heads, then Russia will win.'

'And if it comes out tails?'

'Then Britain will win.'

'Are those the only two alternatives?' askd Hitler anxiously.

'Not at all, the coin could also remain balanced on its side.

'And what would that mean?'

'Then France would win.'

'Is there no other possibility?'

'Of course. Perhaps God will grant a miracle, and the coin will remain suspended in mid-air. Then Czecholovakia will win.'

Party chairman!

'Comrade, why weren't you at the last Party meeting?'

Party member:

'Comrade chairman, if I had known it was the last Party meeting I would definitely have come.'

After the American Civil War, ex-slave Rastus came across his one-time master.

'Hey, boss, now I's a free man, I's as good as you.'

'No you ain't Rastus, 'cos you ain't got a fine big horse like me.'

Rastus worked and saved and bought himself a fine big horse.

'*Now* I's as good as you.'

'No you ain't, Rastus, 'cos you ain't got a beautiful white house on the hill.'

Rastus worked and saved until eventually he too bought a beautiful white house on the hill. Once again he paid a visit to his old master.

'Well boss, *now* I's as good as you. Matter of fact, I's *better* than you.'

'How do you work that out?'

'Well, I's free, I's got a fine big horse, and I's the owner of a beautiful white house on the hill. But *I* ain't got a nigger for a neighbour.'


A Sussex lady sent an invitation to the CO of a newly-arrived American unit:

'Lady Bountiful at home on Saturday, 6-8. Cocktails for twelve of your men. No Jews please.'

On Saturday at 6, twelve pitch-black Negroes arrived on Lady Bountiful's doorstep. She was speechless. At last she stuttered:

'There must be some mistake . . .'

The black sergeant shook his head:

'No, Ma'am. Commander Cohen never makes a mistake . . .'


An old Jew stops in front of a statue of General Moltke in Berlin. A young Nazi is already looking at the statue. Speaking with a strong Yiddish accent, the Jew asks the officer:

'Excuse me, Lieutenant, is this General Moltke?'

'Yes, this is General Moltke,' replies the officer,

sarcastically imitating the man's thick Jewish accent.
The old Jew looks at him reproachfully.
'Why imitate *me*?' he asks. 'Imitate *him*.'


After 1945:
A Pole is asked a difficult question:
'Suppose there was a German and a Russian soldier within the range of your gun, but you have only one bullet, which would you shoot?'
The Pole thinks for a while and says: 'the Russian.'
'Why?'
'Business before pleasure.'


Before 1945:
A Pole is asked a difficult question.
'Suppose there was a German and a Russian soldier within the range of your gun, but you have only one bullet. Which would you shoot?'
The Pole thinks for a while and says: 'The German.'
'Why?'
'Business before pleasure.'


An official from the National Association for the Advancement of Coloured Peoples called in at a city library and asked to see the Chief Librarian.
'There are 10,000 books in this library which contain the word "nigger". I demand that you remove them all from your shelves.'
'Hey, come on,' the Chief Librarian protested, 'there are 50,000 books which contain the word "bastard".'
'Maybe,' the NAACP man replied, 'but you bastards ain't organised yet.'


In Pakistan, three people are brought before a military court for beating up an army major in uniform.
The military judge asks the first man: 'Why did you

beat the major up in public?'

The man answers: 'Because he insulted my wife.'

The second man, when similarly questioned, answers: 'The lady was my sister. I was infuriated.'

The judge turns to the third man: 'And what about you?'

'I was passing by and I saw two men beating up an officer, so I thought martial law was over!'

# 5  *Facts of Life*

*Where do the limits of politics lie? How much of our lives lie beyond its scope? The jokes in this part are about perennial and general features of the human condition which some politicians and creeds may promise to overcome but for which ordinary men and women tend to hold them directly responsible. Perhaps neither view is right, each attributing too great a role to politics. These jokes have an existential quality: and, though rooted in time and place, they convey a general message that is, as always, typically ambivalent.*

---

### 1 Misery

In the era of Johnson's Great Society, the publicity exercise was being conducted the length and breadth of the nation. Somewhere in the Bronx, an enthusiastic official was addressing a large crowd.

'We have announced' – he reaches his rhetorical climax – 'nothing short of an all-out War on poverty!'

At the back of the hall, a lone hand is raised, and a little man speaks up:

'I just want to say one thing – we surrender.'

A young Pakistani civil servant had just got married. He was desperately trying to find somewhere to live. His mother advised him to go and see the *faqir* (holy man) as a last resort. And so he did:

'What I'm looking for is a small apartment, nothing too expensive, just three rooms, kitchen and bathroom, with a balcony and if possible a telephone and . . .'

'Very well,' said the *faqir*. 'Take this incense and burn it in a little blue teapot. A *djinn* will appear, who will make your wish come true.'

The young man did as the *faqir* said. He burned the incense in a little blue teapot. And, sure enough, the *djinn* appeared:

'Your wish is my command!'

'Well, I'd like a small apartment, nothing too expensive, just three rooms, a kitchen and bathroom, with a balcony and if possible a telephone . . .'

'Is that all?' the *djinn* replied. 'You fool! If I had a three-roomed apartment, do you think I'd be living in a teapot?'

An Indian peasant was caught red-handed stealing onions. He is given a choice between paying a hundred rupees, receiving a hundred lashes, or eating a hundred onions.

He chooses the onions, but after about a dozen of them he asks with streaming eyes for the lashes. But after about two dozen of them he finds it too painful and pays the fine. He goes home and tells his wife: 'I really cheated them this time: ate only a few onions, received a number of lashes and . . . delayed the fine as much as I could.'

A prisoner in the Soviet Union is sentenced to be shot. On an icy morning, four soldiers come to take him from his cell, and in driving rain take him by foot to the place of his execution.

After a long walk, the condemned man protests:

'Aren't you ashamed of inflicting this treatment on a man you are about to shoot?'

'What are you complaining about?' replies one soldier, 'we've got to walk back!'

Two Jews sat in a coffeehouse, discussing the fate of their people.

'How miserable is our lot,' said one. 'Poisons, plagues, quotas, discrimination, Hitler, the Klan . . . Sometimes I think we'd be better off if we'd never been born.'

'Sure,' says his friend, 'But who has that much luck? Maybe one in fifty-thousand!'


An elderly man is sitting on a park bench studying a Hebrew book. A KGB agent walks by, looks over the man's shoulder, and says:

'What is that strange writing?'

'This is Hebrew,' says the old man. 'It's the language of Israel.'

'Don't be silly,' says the agent. 'At your age, you'll never get to Israel.'

'Perhaps not,' sighs the old man. 'But Hebrew is also the language of Heaven.'

The agent replies, 'What makes you so sure you're going to Heaven and not to Hell?'

'Maybe I'm not,' says the old man, 'but I already know Russian.'


'What do the Hungarians like about Communism?'

'That the Russians are in it, too.'

*Another version:*

'What is it about Socialism that the Slovaks like best?'

'The fact that the Czechs have to live under it too.'

\*    \*    \*

A Hungarian, whose wife and two daughters had been killed by Russian soldiers during the 1956 uprising, writes to his son, now a refugee in France:

'My dear son. Don't worry about me. Here life is fine and I am very, very happy. Perhaps not as happy as your mother and your sisters, but basically, very, very happy.'

A poor *fellah* (peasant) in Egypt promises his wife to get some food. He goes fishing and after a long while he catches a fat fish. He runs home and tells his wife:
'Here is a fish, grill it!'
'We cannot, no coal!'
Then fry it!'
'No oil!'
'Then boil it!'
'No clean water!'
The *fellah* goes to the Nile and throws the fish back into the water, whereupon the fish jumps out and cries:
'Long live Nasser.'

Heard in the 1930s:
In the desert of Sudan, Levi and Hirsch have met by chance, both carrying heavy loads and followed by a column of porters. There is great rejoicing.
'What are you doing here?'
'I have an ivory cutting factory in Alexandria, and in order to keep down the cost of raw materials, I've decided to shoot the elephants myself. And you?'
'Same thing. I manufacture crocodile skin bags in Port Said and come here to shoot the crocodiles myself.'
'And how is our friend Simon?'
'Oh, He's really adventurous. He's remained in Berlin.'

A man is shipwrecked and finds himself in an uninhabited region. After wandering long in the jungle, he comes at last to a village where he sees a noose from which a corpse is hanging.
'The Lord be praised!' he cries. 'Civilization at last.'

'What is alcoholism?'
'Alcoholism is a transitional stage between capitalism and communism.'

'What is a pessimist?'
'A well-informed optimist.'


'What do Marxist philosophers think of these days?'
'Whether or not there is life before death.'


'Why is General Pinochet called "Hood Robin?" '
'Because he steals from the poor to give to the rich.'

---

## 2 Scarcity

A Polish worker went into a department store in Warsaw.

'Do you sell spare parts for Soviet vacuum cleaners?' he asked the assistant.

'Certainly, comrade,' the assistant replied, producing a broom from behind the counter.


A Budapest restaurant announces that it will guarantee to produce any dish asked for or offer its patrons 100 florins instead. An old tramp, who could do with 100 florins, goes in and orders a plate of giraffe meat and potatoes. The waiter takes the order without batting an eyelid and soon returns with 100 florins on a plate.

'Aha!' says the tramp, 'so you don't have any giraffe meat.'

'Yes, we have plenty,' says the waiter. 'It's potatoes we don't have.'


An official visitor from the Soviet Union is being shown around Budapest. At the end of the tour, he remarks to his Hungarian hosts, 'You must have terrible shortages in this country!'

Astonished, they ask him why he thinks so.

'Because,' he says, 'You have no queues.'

A Polish customer asks his butcher for pork. No luck. Then he asks for beef. Again, no luck. 'What about lamb?' Same answer. 'Any chicken?'

'No.'

'Veal?'

'None.'

He leaves in despair and the butcher turns to his assistant. 'What a fantastic memory!'

'What's fifty metres long and eats potatoes?'

'A queue waiting to buy meat.'

A Rumanian party orator praises the golden future of Communism.

'The party is arranging a revolution in the standard of living. Next year each of you will receive a bicycle, the year after that each a car, the year after that everyone gets a helicopter.'

An elderly worker asks,

'What am I going to do with a helicopter?'

'You idiot,' someone yells. 'You fly to Moscow and see if you can buy some bread!'

Czechoslovakia.

Mr Strougal and Mr Husak see a large queue for meat. 'We haven't got enough meat,' says Strougal.

'*We* have. *They* don't,' says Husak.

A Russian and a Rumanian are having a conversation.

The Russian says, 'All we have to do to deal with the US is pack twenty atomic bombs into leather suitcases and place them strategically in the US.'

The Rumanian shook his head dubiously.

'Don't you believe we have atomic Bombs?' says the Russian.

'Sure, but the problem is where are you going to get twenty leather suitcases?'

'What will Communism be like?'
'Everyone will have what he needs.'
'But what if there's a shortage of meat?'
'Then there'll be a sign in the butchers' saying:
"No meat needed today".'


Vladek is waiting in line for groceries. After five minutes the manager comes out and tells the queue that there's no meat left. After ten minutes he tells them that they've run out of eggs. After half an hour they're told that there are no more vegetables. After an hour they're told that all the bread has gone. When Vladek gets into the store after two hours he's told to go home because there's no food left. He starts cursing and is immediately confronted by a secret police agent who says:
'You know, a few years ago we would have shot people like you: now go home.'
Vladek goes home and tells his wife about how the store ran out of food.
'And you know what?' he said, 'I was lucky, they also ran out of bullets!'


A visitor to Bucharest, seeing a long queue, goes up to the end and asks what people are queuing for. Nobody seems to know, so he works his way to the front and asks the person at the head of the queue, who doesn't know either.
'You see,' he says, 'I was leaning on this wall and I fell asleep. When I woke up, I saw this huge queue behind me, and, since I'd never been at the head of a queue before, I thought I'd stay.'

---

## 3 Work

It is a very hot day in Israel and Chaim and Aharon are sitting on the toilet.
'Chaim,' asks Aharon, 'do you think this is physical

or mental work?'
'I think it must be mental,' replies Aharon.
'Why?' asks Chaim.
'If it were physical I'd hire an Arab to do it.'

A business consultant is cross-examining the top
executives of the National Coal Board in Britain.
'What do you do?' he says to one.
'Nothing.'
Then he asks the next one:
'And what do you do?'
'Nothing.'
'I thought as much,' said the consultant, 'just one
more example of the duplication in this place.'

*Another version*

An efficiency expert was hired to improve the admini-
strative performance of the Jewish Agency in Jerusalem.
He decides to inspect all the offices and arrives one
morning at the Jewish Agency's headquarters.
He opens one door and sees a woman reading the
newspaper *Maariv*.
'What are you doing?'
'Reading a newspaper.'
He opens a second door and sees a man reading
*Maariv*.
'What are you doing?'
'Reading a newspaper.'
He goes out and writes in his notebook:
'Duplication. Both read *Maariv*.'

★   ★   ★

An Englishman, Frenchman and Russian are describing
their wives to each other.
Englishman: 'When my wife rides a horse she reaches
the ground – not because the horse is so short, but
because my wife's legs are so long.'
Frenchman: 'When I embrace my wife I can encircle

her waist with one hand – not because my hand is so big, but because her waist is so slim.'

Russian: 'When I leave home I touch my wife's behind and it keeps trembling until I get back from work – not because she is so fat, but because the work day is so short!'

An American who marries a Rumanian girl goes to work in a factory outside Bucharest. He works hard at his job while the other workers stand idly by. Later when he receives his pay cheque, he notices that he gets the same amount as all the others, so he asks one of them,

'I didn't participate in the strike, why am I getting strike pay?'

The Rumanian worker turns to another and laughs:

'He thinks we are on strike!'

The People's Bicycle Factory in Dresden is celebrating its twentieth anniversary.

The director gives a speech. He congratulates the workforce, which has trebled in size since the factory opened. He welcomes representatives of the Party, the Government and the Volksarmee. Finally, with considerable emotion, he brings on to the stage the factory's very first customer – an old man who, twenty years ago, brought a bicycle chain in for repair. Ushered to the microphone, the old man expresses his heartfelt thanks for the honour done to him. Concluding his little speech, he turns to the director:

'There's just one more thing, Comrade. Could you tell me when my bicycle chain will be ready for collection?'

'When I came home from the factory last night, I found my wife in bed with another man. How can I prevent that happening again?'

'Work more overtime.'

'Why don't Hungarian workers ever go on strike?'
'Because no one would notice the difference.'
'And why don't Hungarian workers ever work?'
'It's a tradition in Hungary. The ruling class never works.'
'So why is everyone so happy?'
'Because the workers behave as if they worked, and the employers behave as if they paid.'

A civil servant is badly hurt falling down the stairs of the Ministry, and he is taken to the hospital where he remains unconscious for several days. Finally, an eye opens and his doctor tells him:
'My friend, I have good news and bad news for you. First of all, you'll never be able to work again.'
'And now,' says the wounded civil servant, 'tell me the bad news.'

A brutal murderer is sentenced to death by hanging. Reading of the court's decision, Hitler irately turns to Goering:
'A swift death is too good for a criminal like that. He ought to be made to starve to death slowly and agonizingly.' Whereupon Goering replies,
'How about opening a small shop for him?'

---

## 4 Corruption

A competition was once held to establish which was the most corrupt country on earth. To the astonishment of its citizenry, Mexico only took second place. After a time, and explanation emerged. The Mexican authorities had bribed the judges.

In Egypt a man approached the Minister of Commerce and asked for a licence.

'I will pay you 200 lira if you grant me this licence,' said the man to the Minister, 'and nobody will know about it.'

'Give me 1,000 lira and you can tell everyone,' replies the Minister.


A Russian Minister visits a car factory.

The Manager goes out of his way to show him around and at the end of the tour offers the Minister a free car.

'Oh no,' says the Minister, 'I cannot accept it.'

'In that case I'll sell it to you for five roubles.'

The Minister hands him a bill of ten roubles: 'In that case, I'll have two.'


Following an Irish election a voter approached his local MP to try to get a government appointment. He reminded the candidate:

'I voted for Your Honour under thirteen different names, and I couldn't have done more for you than that, could I?'


Sadat and his cabinet were in Upper Egypt conferring with Kissinger. Someone phoned from Cairo to tell him that his palace had been burgled and everything in it stolen.

'Wait a minute,' says Sadat and goes to the other room. He returns after a while and shouts into the receiver:

'Impossible. I have all the Ministers here with me.'


Danny Morrison, prominent Northern Ireland Sinn Fein spokesman:

'Sinn Fein will come to power in Ireland with an Armalite in one hand, and a ballot paper in the other.'

Said of Pat O'Conner, C.J. Haughey's election agent, who was charged with personation in the general election February 1982:

'Fianna Fáil will come to power in Ireland with a ballot paper in one hand – and a ballot paper in the other.'

A Soviet Minister, finding that his son was not shaping very well at the college for top people's children, sent him to a careers adviser who reported:

'Your vocational aptitude test indicates that your future lies in the ministry which is run by your father.'

Starace and Farinacci, two big Italian fascist top-brasses, see a 1000 lire note on the pavement; both run for it and start arguing as to who should keep it. Finally, Farinacci says:

'All right, let's give it to a charitable institution.'

Starace hesitates and then says,

'No, there's no point in making it go the usual round; let's just share it now.'

*Another version*

Nazi Germany.

Two full-time Party officials go for a walk and one finds a 50 mark note in the gutter. The other asks what he intends to do with it.

'Donate it to the Winter Relief,' he proclaims.

'But why,' asks his friend, 'do it the long way round?'

\*   \*   \*

Guha went out with his friends for a trip. When they reached the lake they saw the Imam drowning.

Everyone started to shout:

'Your holiness, give us your hand, give your hand.'

But the Imam didn't hear them and was sinking fast.

Then Guha walked to the bank of the lake and cried:

'Take my hand! Take my hand!'

Presently the Imam extended his hand and Guha took

him out of the water.

Everybody gathered around Guha:

'Tell us, how come he heard you and couldn't hear us?'

'Simple, my friends,' said Guha, 'I know the Imam, he only knows how to take and you wanted him to give.'

## 5 Relativity

Two Jews come to the rabbi with a cow.

Says the first: 'This is my cow. I can describe all its qualities.'

The rabbi: 'I believe that you are right.'

Says the second: 'This is my cow and I can bring many witnesses to prove it.'

The rabbi: 'I believe you are right.'

The rabbi's wife who heard it comes to him and says: 'But rabbi, there is only one cow and they cannot both be right.'

The rabbi turns to her: 'You are right, too!'

*Another version:*

The Mullah Nasrudin was made a magistrate. During his first case the plaintiff argued so persuasively that he exclaimed:

'You are right!'

The clerk of the court begged him to restrain himself, for the defendant had not been heard yet.

Nasrudin was so carried away by the eloquence of the defendant that he cried out as soon as the man had finished his evidence:

'You are right!'

The clerk of the court could not allow this.

'Your honour, they cannot *both* be right.'

'I believe you are right!' said Nasrudin.

\*   \*   \*

A Hungarian refugee who is living unhappily in London

is asked why he does not return to his country:

'I am like a diver who is searching for the remains of a wreckage at the bottom of the ocean. Suddenly I hear the voice of the Captain from the ship above saying: "Come up quickly now!" '

'Why?'

'Because the ship is sinking!'

During the First World War a regiment of Talmudic scholars was conscripted into the Tsarist army. The scholars proved to be excellent marksmen, with a sure eye and a steady hand. In rifle-practice they invariably hit the target with every shot they fired.

They were immediately sent to the Galician front. As the Austrian troops advanced towards the Russian lines, they were ordered to fire. Nothing happened. The commanding officer of the regiment grabbed the Talmudic scholar nearest to him and screamed:

'WHY THE HELL DON'T YOU SHOOT!'

The scholar turned round in shocked amazement:

'But those are *men* out there!'

Battle was about to be joined. The Tsarist officer strutted up and down in front of his troops.

'Right, men,' he ordered, fix your bayonets. The fighting will be man-to-man.'

'Would you mind showing me now which is my man?' Private Goldberg asked. 'Perhaps we can come to some arrangement.'

The Mullah hears a commotion in the street outside his house in the middle of the night. His wife tells him to go down and after many arguments, he puts a blanket on his shoulders and goes down to the street. There were many people in the street and a lot of noise, and in the crowd somebody steals his blanket. The Mullah goes home and his wife asks him:

'What was that all about?'
'It seems to be about my blanket.'


The South African Van der Merwe was given the job of showing an important Russian visitor over his plant.

'How it it,' asked the Russian, 'that your output has gone down so much more this year than last?'

'Ah, strikes,' said Van, 'we had twenty recently.'

'Ah, we do not have strikes,' smiled the Russian. 'We do not allow strikes, our workers toe the line . . .'

'Maybe,' said Van, 'but then you don't have to contend with blerry Communists like these rooineks.'


An American and a Rumanian are discussing laissez-faire.

American: 'A worker earns $250 a month, and spends $200.

Rumanian: 'What does he do with the rest?'

American: 'That's his own business. Nobody interferes in such matters.'

Rumanian: 'A worker earns 700 lei and spends about 1400.'

American: 'How does he get the rest?'

Rumanian: 'That's his own business. Nobody interferes in such matters.'


A Jew is travelling with a Chinaman. The Chinaman asks:

'How many Jews are there in the world?'

'Oh, some 12–15 million.'

'And how many Chinese are there?'

'Oh, some 800 million.'

'That's funny. We don't seem to see many of you around.'


A Martian from outer space was greatly attracted by a

traffic light. Finally he summons the courage to hug it and was baffled to see the signal change from 'go' to 'stop'. 'American women are all teases,' he says in dismay.

Papadopoulos was trying to run the whole country. He appointed himself President, Vice-President, Minister of Defence, Minister of the Economy, and the like.

Meanwhile, the Chinese government sent a new ambassador to Greece. The new Chinese ambassador had to meet the President, the Vice-President, and then all the Ministers of the various government departments.

After his first two days in Athens, he told his aide:

'I am really confused! They say that all Chinese look alike, but all the Greek officials that I meet here look the same to me!'

Standing on Lenin's tomb in Red Square, Stalin was acknowledging the acclamation of the masses. Suddenly he raised his hands to silence the crowd.

'Comrades!' he cried. 'A most historic event! A telegram of congratulations from Leon Trotsky!'

The crowd could hardly believe its ears. It waited in hushed anticipation.

'Joseph Stalin,' read Stalin. 'The Kremlin. Moscow. You were right and I was wrong. You are the true heir of Lenin. I must apologise. Trotsky.'

A roar erupted from the crowd.

But in the front row a little Jewish tailor gestured frantically to Stalin.

'Psst!' he cried. 'Comrade Stalin!'

Stalin leaned over to hear what he had to say.

'Such a message! But you read it without the right *feeling*.'

Stalin once again raised his hands to still the excited crowd.

'Comrades!' he announced. 'Here is a simple worker,

a Communist, who says that I did not read Trotsky's message with the right *feeling*. I ask that worker to come up on to the podium himself to read Trotsky's telegram.'

The tailor jumped up on to the podium and took the telegram into his hands. He read:

'Joseph Stalin. The Kremlin. Moscow.'

Then he cleared his throat and sang out:

'You were *right* and I was *wrong*? *You* are the true heir of Lenin? *I* should *apologise*?'


A poor man becomes desperate and decides to write a letter to God, and ask him for £100. He writes a letter addressed to God and posts it and when it arrives at the post office they don't know what to do with it.

They open the letter and when they realize the terrible condition of the poor man they decide to collect money among themselves and send it to him. They manage to collect only £10 and they send it to the poor man. When the poor man receives the letter with the money he sits to write another letter to God:

'Dear God, thank you very much for the money, but please, next time don't send it through the post: they stole £90.'

---

## 6 Time

A Czech goes to a palm reader:

The palmist: 'I see in your hand that now . . .'

The Czech: 'Please, skip the present.'


A Party commission was holding an on-the-spot investigation into technological progress in Hungarian agriculture. The Commission interviewed a peasant on an outlying farm:

'What sort of harvest have you had this year?'

'Average.'

'What does that mean?'
'A little worse than last year, a little better than next.'


God Almighty summons his Thurbar (congregation of rulers).
The Ayatollah Khomeini cries:
'We have so many problems in Iran. O Almighty Allah! When will our problems come to an end?'
'Not in your lifetime,' the Almighty replies.
Then General Zia of Pakistan cries out:
'We have terrible problems in Pakistan. O Almighty Allah! When will the problems in my country be solved?'
'Not in my lifetime,' replies the Almighty.


*Another version:*

Kennedy comes to God and says:
'Tell me, God, how many years before my people will be happy?'
'Fifty years,' God replies.
Kennedy weeps and leaves.
De Gaulle comes to God and asks:
'Tell me, God, how many years before my people are happy?'
'A hundred years,' replies God.
De Gaulle weeps and leaves.
Khruschev comes to God and says:
'Tell me God, how many years before my people will be happy?'
God weeps and leaves.

&#42;   &#42;   &#42;

A Southern Congressman was interviewed on his eightieth birthday.
'You've been on Congress a long time, haven't you, sir?' the reporter asked.
'Ah sure have. Comin' up forty-five years.'
'And you must have seen some mighty big changes,

right, sir?'
'Yeah,' the old man replied gruffly, 'an' Ah've voted against 'em all.'


What is the difference between a fairy story in the East and a fairy story in the West?
Fairy stories in the West start with the words 'Once upon a time there was . . .' Fairy stories in the East begin with the words 'Once upon a time there will be . . .'


A man walked into the waiting room of a government department in Prague. He turned to another man sitting in the corner.
'Is it a long wait?'
'I couldn't say. I'm new here myself. I've only been waiting two months.'


Czechoslovakia 1970:
'What is black and knocking at the door?'
'The Future.'


Sign in Montreal: 'Remember the good old days when sex was dirty and the air was clean.'


The future is certain: only the past is unpredictable.


## 7 War and peace

Eisenhower: 'I'm a little worried about the tension in Berlin, John.'
Dulles (alarmed): 'Why? Is it relaxing?'

In the jungles of Vietnam an American patrol stops to size up the situation.

'Sarge!' says one of the soldiers, 'we have the enemy in front of us.'

'Sarge,' says another, 'we have enemy troops to the left!'

'Sarge, we have enemy troops to the right.'

'Sarge, we have enenmy troops behind us!'

'Good,' says the Sergeant. 'We've finally caught them.'

'How many atom-bombs would you need to destroy France?' asked General Haig's son.

'France?' said Haig. 'I really don't know, son. Why, thirty or forty, I should imagine.'

'And Britain?'

'Hard to say, son. Twenty-five – thirty. Or perhaps forty.'

'And the US?'

'Can't say I ever really thought about it. Fifty or sixty. Or even eighty, maybe.'

'And the Soviet Union?'

'Ninety-three, son.'

A conversation between two Soviet Jews after the Six Day War:

'Hey! Did you hear how we beat us?'

An Egyptian felt the need of a brain transplant and walking into a surgical supply store asked what they had in the way of brains. He was shown the brain of an excellent mathematician who had died the year before at the age of sixty. In view of its age, he could have it for five hundred dollars.

The Egyptian felt the age was a disadvantage. 'Do you have anything younger?' he asked.

A peasant's brain was shown him. He had died at the age of twenty-five.

The Egyptian shook his head. He was a little too high-class for a peasant's brain. 'What is this one?' he said suddenly, for one brain was encased in a beautiful glass-walled refrigerator with a spotlight on it.

'That,' said the dealer, 'is our prize possession. It is the brain of an Egyptian general who died fighting gallantly against Israel, and it costs a hundred thousand dollars.'

'A hundred thousand dollars!' said the would-be customer, shocked. 'Why so much?'

And the dealer said, 'Because it's never been used.'

Two Egyptian officers are talking.

'What a pity the war ended on the sixth day,' says one. 'One more day and we would have occupied the whole of Libya.'

During the Six Day War, President Brezhnev telephones President Nasser to ask:

'Would you like us to send you the next batch of Soviet planes, or shall we destroy them on the ground?'

A Mexican to an Argentinian: 'My very deep sympathies . . . You do not know how sorry I am that things went as they did in the Malvinas.

Argentinian: 'Why be sorry? It is the first time we entered a war and we came in second. That is not bad . . .'

'Why has President Galtieri ordered a glass-bottomed boat?'

'So he can inspect his airforce.'

1916. A German guard is talking to a Russian prisoner-of-war.

'Kaiser Wilhelm is a great man. He visits the front once a week.'

'Our Tsar Nicholas is even greater. He stands on a spot twenty miles behind the lines, and every week the front goes to meet him.'


'What is the difference between Chamberlain and Hitler?'
'One takes a weekend in the country, while the other takes a country in a weekend.'


On the occasion of his fiftieth birthday, the National Socialist motorcycle corps are making Hitler a present of movable frontier posts.


Can Germany lose the war?
Unfortunately not, now we've got it, we'll never get rid of it.


A Czech teacher is discussing heroism and asks the class for examples.
A little boy puts his hand up:
'The other week I was out walking and I heard some screams and I saved a little girl from drowning.'
The teacher says: 'Very good, Josef, but I don't think we should mention ourselves in this connection.'
A second little boy volunteers:
'Last summer we were on holiday, the house next door caught fire and my father saved our neighbour's family single-handed.'
The teacher says:
'Admirable, Franz, but that fire was purely accidental. We must find an instance that shows a deeper level of ideological commitment.'
A third little boy speaks up:
'My father, during the last war, was in the front line and shot down an entire company of the enemy, all by himself.'

The teacher was delighted.

'Excellent, Jiri, now let us explore this case in more detail. First, what was your father's rank?'

'Obersturmführer.'

At a reception for Politburo members at the Soviet General Staff headquarters, a marshal suddenly shouts: 'Who pressed the white button, who pressed the white button?'

He is beside himself with rage when no one answers. The marshal downs another vodka, wipes the perspiration from his face and, with a casual wave of the hand, says: 'Well, after all – who really cares about Albania?'

An elderly lady meets a senior police officer at a social gathering and asks him in what campaign he earned the medal he is wearing.

'That's a Socialist award,' he says, 'and I got it for my services in peacetime.'

'I see,' said the old lady. 'I quite forgot that the Vopo (People's Police) also shoot at civilians.'


Two Jews were serving in the Russian Army during the First World War. One day their unit had to cross a bridge and they were sent on a reconnaissance mission. They crawled gently to the bridge, inspected it thoroughly and reported back to their commander:

'The artillery will pass the bridge, no doubt about that.'

'The cavalry – maybe.'

'The infantry – definitely not.'

'How is this possible?' asks the commander. 'Artillery yes and infantry no?'

'You see, there are two big dogs on the other side of the bridge!'


A man argues bitterly with his wife. Seeing this, a friend of the husband reasons with him:

'I don't understand you,' he says. 'In my household we never argue because everything is regulated once and for all. I make the important decisions and my wife looks after the details.'

'But how do you decide which is which?' asks the first.

'It's simple. My wife decides about the children's schooling, the doctor who treats them, where we take out holidays, what kind of car we have etc . . . These are the details. And I decide whether England should enter the Common Market, whether the franc should be revalued, whether the US should leave Vietnam.'

The workers from a factory complained one day to Hitler that they always had to stand in the background when all the big-wigs stood in the front, to be seen by the Fuhrer. Hitler reassured them,

'Just wait until I wage my war; then you'll all be at the front and all the big-wigs will be in the background.'

Picasso is summoned by the Nazi commandant of Paris who shows him a reproduction of his famous painting of Guernica's destruction by German bombers in the Spanish Civil War.

'Did you do that?' the commandant asks the artist in a menacing tone.

'No,' replies Picasso. 'You did.'

'Will there be a Third World War?'

'No, but there will be such a struggle for peace that not a stone will be left standing.'

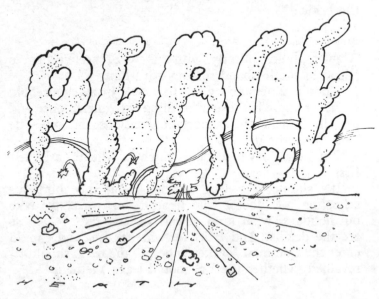

# Index